CW00421948

BANDS,
BOOZE
AND
BALLROOMS

by

Dorothea Desforges

Published by Buttercup Press,
South Cave, East Yorkshire, HU15 2JG

©Dorothea Desforges 2001

All rights reserved

ISBN 0-9539190-6-4

Typeset by Gem Desk Top Publishing
Welton, East Yorkshire, HU15 1NP

Printed by Central Print Services
The University of Hull

INTRODUCTION

This book is a testimonial to many fine musicians who gave so much pleasure to dancers during the twentieth century.

Names like *Harry Chatterton, Tommy Fisher, Leslie Rose* and *Bill Kinsey* are synonymous with the ballrooms and dance halls of East Yorkshire.

Memories come and memories go but the dancing years will live forever in our hearts.

I have tried to do justice to the durability of an era, attempting to include as many bands and musicians as possible, relevant to the period.

Some musicians were asked to recall incidents from over sixty years ago, but I'm afraid with the frailty of age, some names and venues were elusive, even with photographs, so a few local 'names' may have inadvertently been missed out. But regardless of the passage of time we have attempted to be as accurate as possible - Honest.

ACKNOWLEDGEMENTS

Thank you to all the musicians and their partners who helped me compile this book of nostalgia.

I hope I have included most of the significant bands and musicians prevalent in the dancing years, but memory does tend to select only the very interesting and the disreputable - I'm pleased to say.

I was loaned treasured photographs, which persuaded many of you to retrace steps thought long forgotten. But I'm sure we missed a few personnel out or put you in the wrong place at the wrong time - if so, sorry, but well meaning as my informants were, sentiment does sometimes encroach on actual fact.

I enjoyed meeting you and hearing your entertaining, risquè and evocative memories.

Without doubt, they are the most compelling reasons I know to, 'keep music live.'

Some of my favourite musical quotes:

Louis Armstrong: "There's only two ways to sum up music: either it's good or it's bad. If it's good you don't mess with it; you just enjoy it."

Music can be made anywhere, it's invisible and it does not smell (W. H. Auden 1951)

I believe that the use of noise to make music will continue and increase until we reach a music produced through the aid of electrical instruments. That was written by John Cake in 1937

Show me an orchestra that likes the conductor and I'll show you a lousy orchestra.

When someone asked Jazzman *Duke Ellington* about musicians, he replied: "Some musicians play 99 per cent of the instrument and sound wonderful, some play ten per cent of the instrument but what they do with that ten per cent, no one else in the world can achieve."

CONTENTS

FOREWORD

Bands, Booze and Ballrooms is like a scrapbook full of photographs, incidents and anecdotes which will unlock a door of reminiscences. It's a nostalgic peep into yesteryear, depicting the dance band period in Hull and East Yorkshire, but it could be anywhere. The same scenario was being played throughout the country.

Recall the catchy tunes and melodies that evoke the memory of the ballroom. Nothing stirs the memory like a song.

We stroll through the years of strict tempo, rock and roll, jive and the twist. Evocative recollections and eye witness accounts from the musicians of the day.

Lost teeth, dead cows, mutes in places mutes shouldn't be, lost music, forgotten music and somebody else's music. Maverick trumpeters, delirious drummers and completely mad band leaders. It's all here and I think most of the stories will trigger some personal recollections - if not, it will capture the imagination.

The long list of dance hall which proliferated throughout the region are now either derelict, been pulled down or turned into bingo halls and trendy wine bars. For this generation the book is a guide to part of our history.

It does not give the complete story, but I hope it touches on the significant factors of the dance band era. That era is gone, but not forgotten - yet. They say you should not look back but if you do the view opens and the true scale and importance of it grows clearer. In fact the sweet pain of nostalgia is one of the great pleasures of life.

Some names have been changed to protect the innocent. Innocent? Musicians?! Ha! Read on.

BANDS,

BOOZE

AND

BALLROOMS

A nostalgic look at the dance band era.

Ambrose Gibbins Orchestra 1932: Piano: Ambrose Gibbins - Trumpet: Bill Clutterbrook - Sax's: Ken Asquith, George Spicer - Clarinet: Bill Conyers - Double Bass: Frank Taylor - Drums: Ernest Scarr

Loaned to me by Ambrose Gibbins' widow, showing the boys at Aldbrough. They'd cycled there for a gig.

A FEW ODDMENTS TO
WHET YOUR APPETITE

Have you ever thought how beginners practise their instrument and still stay friends with neighbours? When *Timothy West* needed to acquire some trumpet skills for a BBC documentary, he said he started in the middle of summer, when everyone had their windows open but after a number of complaints he decided to drive to Wimbledon Common. He sat down on a log in the middle of some dense undergrowth and started to play his trumpet. But it was not to be, as soon as he started a stranger appeared and told him music was forbidden, so he had to go. Eventually he found a cart track and as he drove down it he came across stubble of a newly harvested field and there was able to practise to his hearts content.

But I liked the story about a Hull musician, *Wilf Moran*. He worked on coasters and said he used to take his trumpet to sea with him and practise in the engine room. One night they were travelling in thick fog and the Captain kept slowing down because he thought the noises he heard were other ship's blowing their fog horns. But every time he slowed down to listen, Wilf kept quiet, then when they started up again, off he'd go.

A musician was walking home after a gig in Scarborough and ended up being arrested by the constabulary. "There I was walking along quietly with my instrument tucked under my arm, when this policeman pulled up and said he was nicking me for robbery. I pleaded my innocence, but the policeman said he'd just heard about it on his radio. Evidently the victim had given chase but the thief had tucked the 'goods' under his arm and legged it, giving him the slip.

The copper wasn't convinced by my story, so radioed in to check the details. It made my night when I heard them say to him: "No you silly sod, we didn't say a saxophone had been nicked we said a fax and phone."

Eric Wright said they used to play on the Yorkshireman that plied punters across the Humber. "It would make ten or twelve crossings a day and we would charge 3d (just over a penny) for them to come in for a dance. We were making a fortune."

Which reminds me of a story told to me by **Mike Pinfold**, author of that excellent book 'The Big Band Years.'
"Riverboat shuffles abounded along the Humber Estuary in the sixties. On one infamous occasion discarded beer bottles, shied from the lower deck by over-relaxed revellers, caused the ferry Captain consternation when the floating objects pock-marked his radar screen."

My friend Muriel asked me if she could borrow one of my long dresses to go to a dance. It was white, with short, puff sleeves. She noticed the hairs on her arms seemed to be more prominent against the white, so her sister advised, 'rub pumice stone on them, they'll disappear like magic.' She did, but the morning of the dance her arms were red raw. She tried to get some long white gloves to cover them up, but not a shop in Hull had any in stock, so she decided to bind them both with bandages and pretended she'd fallen and scraped the skin off. Well it was half right!

A keyboard player was asked if he could go along with a trio to play a few tunes to an old peoples home.
When they were introduced the Chairwoman said: "Now you all know we normally have an intelligent speaker for our Thursday afternoon get-togethers, but today we thought we'd have a change."

What would we do without those redoubtable chairmen/women?
John Mallinder told me: "Sounds Easy had been booked to play for the annual dance at a West Yorkshire Working Men's Club. We were all set up and ready to start when the typical Chairman decided it was he and he alone who should make the announcements. During the evening he must have introduced

us at least eight times and never got our name right once. That was in spite of the fact we had five stands at the front, all with our name prominently displayed."

The boys were discussing **Bernard Collinson**, when **Ray DesForges** recalled a telephone conversation with him: "He rang and offered me his mouthpiece. 'I know you like it Ray,' he told me, 'but I've only got two months to live, so I want you to have it. What the hell do you say to something like that?" he asked

"Did I tell you about the dance band vocalist who missed a three gigs because the dog ate his false teeth?" asked Keith.
"No," I said eagerly. "Name names."
He just tapped the side of his nose and told me, "That's for me to know and you to find out."
Spoilsport!
But he did go on to tell me about the vocalist who would disappear after each song, the band would play a couple of numbers then he'd be back on stage to do his stuff. Except he was already doing it - in the dressing room with a girl.
"And don't you go thinking it's only the fellah's," said Keith, "I know of a girl vocalist who went missing after a spot and the band leader muttered to me to go find her. I did - spread-eagled across a table in the back with the M.C."
No wonder he wouldn't name names. But it certainly adds spice to musician's get-togethers.

George Wilcox told me that he was in a band which was playing on a live recording for the British Forces Broadcasting Service and they had Alfred Marks as a comic and the vocalist was **Dusty Springfield**. "The 'stars' had to walk down a sloping ramp to get to the microphone. Our baritone was a huge man, who when he sat down, completely obliterated the seat. As *Alfred Marks* passed him he couldn't resist grabbing a fistful of that hanging flesh. Millions of listeners must have wondered what was happening as the sax player let out a horrendous scream. They never were told. But I expect they'd guess nobody was getting murdered as the whole audience had seen what had happened and were convulsed with ribald laughter. Quite made the show."

Keith Parker joined in, telling me about the trumpeter **Pete Dawson**, who had been asked to augment on the Billy Smart's Circus band as it paraded through the streets of Hull.

"He'd been playing a gig the night before and got chatting up this girl. He told her to stand at the corner of Ferensway so he'd see her. Sure enough the girl was dutifully stood on the pavement and Pete was blowing his heart out to impress his new lady friend, except the band had turned right and Pete carried straight on. I don't think the elephants got a look in after that," said Keith.

I think one of my favourite stories is about a quartet, which had been booked to liven up the day at a nursing home. "Entertaining the elderly can be tricky," said the vocalist. "If they don't know the song they all start talking. But on this occasion this was the least of our problems.

Halfway through the show, I was well into 'Underneath the Arches,' when an old dear in the front gave a sort of deep breath and lolled quietly over to her left. No one realised at first what had happened, until she toppled onto the floor.

"There followed a riotous pantomime while staff attempted to lift the recently departed from the floor, they obviously weren't going to drag her out by her ankles, as that would allow the rest of the other oldies to cotton to the fact she wasn't taking her afternoon siesta. So the corpse was placed on a bed in a side-room awaiting the arrival of a doctor who was needed to confirm death. A confused individual called Mrs Norris usually occupied the room. Now Mrs Norris was a tough old bird, but her mind had gone. She evidently answered any conversation or attempted conversation with the same phrase, which was "I wish I was your age."

Mrs Norris was at that time watching our show. But she got bored - Not quite as bored as the other lady, but none-the-less bored - In fact she became so bored she decided to leave the room. But the staff didn't notice as they were on the phone to the doctor, so she sloped back unnoticed.

When the doctor arrived, Mrs Norris was sitting happily up in bed and the corpse was now lying face down on the floor. The old bird nodded in her direction "I wish I was her age," she muttered.

Later when the band were talking about the demise of the lady, the drummer commented, "Now that's what I call a critic."

Drummers. You either love 'em or hate 'em. I once saw a drummer wearing a tee shirt, which read "Let me take you dancing in the isles."

"It's from Hawaii," he told me, gave me a cheeky wink and continued: "One good lei and I'm anybody's!"

David Alderson, a big band enthusiast, has always loved that type of music, but has found it increasingly hard over the years to persuade his wife to share his passion. "As a birthday surprise for her I'd booked tickets for a big band concert in Leeds," said David, "We'd just got out of the car and were heading for the venue when she suddenly turned to me and said, 'I hope there isn't any drum solos in this concert. I hate them'. We were going to a *Buddy Rich* concert!"

Which leads me on to another story told by *Keith Parker*.

"John, a drummer, was fed up of being told that "anyone can play the drums" and decided to try some other instruments.

He went into a music shop and said to the assistant: "I'll take that red trumpet over there and the accordion in the corner."

"Well," replied a confused assistant, "You can have the fire extinguisher, but the radiators have got to stay."

Naughty, naughty Keith.

The late *Ronnie Scott*, was famous for his one-liners and often it was the poor old drummers who were the butt of the jazz musician's humour. Example:

"Mr Scott, when I grow up, I want to be a musician."

"That's good, what do you want to play?"

"The drums."

"Make up your mind son you can't be both."

My friend Melanie, blonde and very pretty, played the drums. She told me, "During one gig in Leeds I'd noticed a young man giving me the eye. As we were packing up he walked up to me and I thought he was going to offer to help, but instead he asked me. "Do you have to have strong arms to play the drums?" I told him. "Sort of, but it's not important. Why, do you want to be a drummer?"

"No," he said, " It's just that you've got the biggest forearms I've ever seen on a woman," then walked off."

Bands often have to book a 'dep' when they are ill or on holiday. *Bill Kinsey* had booked a deputy drummer for a week. It wasn't a musician the boys were familiar with, but the young man was eager to please, "What do you like to hear from drummers?"

"As little as possible." he was told.

Mike Pinfold says he recalls an American drummer who was headlining at the London Palladium but he was not up to standard. "The audience were letting him know in no uncertain terms so he suddenly stood up and shouted 'Any of you limeys who'd like to take me on I'll see you outside.' He then stormed off the stage."

At an out of town band were playing a gig in Hull. At the end of the night they told the manager they wanted another twenty pounds and they threatened to smash the piano if he didn't pay up.

The manager told me: "As it was on loan from Gough & Davy, I thought I'd better pay up. Gough's got their piano back in one piece and I'd learnt a salutary lesson. It was going to be local bands from then on. I wouldn't mind but they were bloody awful."

Paul Shepherdson went one better. "At the end of one gig the organiser said he hadn't enough money to pay us. A lot of the audience were still in the hall so they had a whip round. The guy collected it in a bucket and said he'd pop to the loo to sort it out. We cleared our gear and the audience was well gone. We hung around then the bass player went to find him, but he'd done a bunk. We never did get paid."

Another story from Paul: "I knew a musician who'd been asked to get a band together to do some gigs in Germany. Problem was he never met them until they were on the boat going over. On the first night he didn't need telling the drummer was a waste of time. The management insisted he got another. He did - and another and another and another. Six in all. He couldn't wait to get home."

The playwright, *Alan Plater* is a well-documented lover of jazz. He's such a familiar figure in Ronnie Scott's he has his own special table.

He told me when he was younger, it was his ambition to learn an instrument and play in a band. "When I was about fifteen years old I bought a cheap guitar. I found out it was cheap because it had an accident and the bridge had been put back in the wrong place. It was one note short of an octave. But I persevered and eventually with a couple of school mates, we managed to learn three songs, well three and a half actually, so we decided it was time to do a gig at school. It had to be one of the three most humiliating times of my life."

I brightened visibly. "Tell me more."

"No chance. I think it's fair to say the other two are my secrets and none of your business."

Ah, well, you can't win 'em all.

Talking about jazz, I was listening to a radio-talk in programme and a listener rang in to say. "I love jazz, when I feel depressed I always put on a *Cleo Laine* record."

The presenter, *Peter Adamson*, a noted music lover himself, was impressed and said: "I'm going to take an educated guess here and have switched the order round a bit. What would you say to a bit of *Tony Bennett*?"

"Oh, God, I can't stand him," said the woman.

The late *Roy Castle* a talented musician told me when he was at the start of his career and appearing with the incomparable *Jimmy James* in Blackpool, they were on the bill with two Yorkshire lads. "One was the Withernsea trumpeter *Kenny Baker* and the other, Hull vocalist *David Whitfield*. Roy said: "Kenny wowed them every night with his rendition of 'Carnival in Venice and it was a fiendishly difficult number."

Harry Chatterton's wife Doreen told me Kenny started his career with Chat's band.

I met the broadcaster *David Jacobs*, while he was compering a show in Leeds. He told me about the time that he was asked to introduce Frank Sinatra at the Royal Festival hall. "I knocked at the dressing room door and his black valet answered, I said: 'Hello, I'm David Jacobs and I'm here to escort Mr Sinatra to the stage'. He looked me over carefully then said, 'I'm Mr Jacobs as well, do you think we could be related?! I was ushered inside the dressing room and Mr Sinatra was stood on a table, clad only in his socks, shirt and his boxer shorts - His valet took a pair of black trousers off a nearby hanger and the singer gingerly put them on, assisted by Mr Jacobs. Stepping down, the valet placed Frank's ramrod arms into the evening jacket. I led him to the stage and wondered why he was walking so stiffly, so asked him. He gave me a cursory glance and told me, "Because I don't want to appear in a crumpled suit like you."

Have you ever seen David Jacobs anything but the epitome of sartorial elegance? David went on: "He can't have been too perturbed as the next time I was in Palm Springs, he invited me to his home and I spent a very pleasurable few hours in his company."

A trumpeter had been playing on board a boat berthed in King George Dock. As usual drink was free and plentiful. After the interval he started arguing forcibly with the bandleader, who told him to 'get lost'. The musician was so furious he went backstage, stripped off and paraded naked through the ship. He was arrested and I'm told he was put in irons for the night to cool down.

Playing for a wedding party can cause a few headaches, said *Ray Desforges*, "if only for the fact that itinerant sheep can keep wandering in the marquee and leaving their calling cards."

A married musician, who shall be nameless, had been visiting his girlfriend who lived above a barber's shop. As he left he decided it would be the perfect alibi to have a haircut, so in he went. The barber had beautifully shorn his left side and was setting about the back when the door opened and in walked his father-in-law. The musician was mortified. George was behind him asking for an appointment, so while he was otherwise occupied, the musician whipped off his cape, slapped a fiver on the shelf in front and sidled out. Luckily he lived to tell me the tale.

LET'S FACE THE MUSIC AND DANCE

We have lived through a century of dramatic change. Horses ploughed the fields, indoor plumbing was unheard of and most children left school at fourteen. During the 1900's we had conscription and steam locomotives. Very few people owned cars, so if you missed the bus, you had to walk.

The ballroom came into its own in the twenties when the Licensing Act of 1921 allowed drinks to be served after 11pm providing food was served. Everybody tried to get in on the dancing craze and to take advantage of the new laws, they situated tables around a dance floor.

Bert Ambrose used to instruct his orchestra, "Never play so loudly that we cannot hear the swish of the frocks as they dance past."

But for most of the population a night out usually meant the pub, the cinema or the theatre, as variety was alive and well. Although money was tight in the 1940's a quarter of the population visited the cinema twice a week, but during the 50's and 60's a new Britain was emerging and the dance hall with its mandatory spinning ball, came into it's own. Quicksteps, waltzes and fox-trots were the most popular, but no evening would be complete without skipping around to the St. Bernard Waltz, Valeta, Military Two-Step and the Gay Gordons, interspersed with a tango or two.

After a dance, a gang of us would often be arm in arm, laughing and singing, with friends peeling off as they came to their street. None of us drank, well nothing more sinister than lemonade anyway, with maybe one or two brave souls sampling a Babycham. One, we couldn't afford it - well the dance did cost 5/- (about 15p) - and two, we were having a whale of a time without it. I had a seven-mile walk home, but never thought anything of it, even in the pouring rain.

Everyone got dressed in his or her Sunday best. The boys usually only owned one suit, which was always pressed before going out.

I can still remember how excited I felt every Wednesday and Saturday knowing I was going dancing. Most of us made our own clothes and in the 50's, the wide, circular skirts, with miles and miles of tulle underskirt making them stand to attention were all the fashion. Girls rustled as they walked. I once bought a pair of gold, hoop earrings, but had to put them on at the dance, as my parents did not approve of such fripperies. I was twenty years old! Make-up was equally frowned upon, so we made it simple with a bit of Pond's vanishing cream, some loose powder and a smattering of Cover Girl lipstick. Hair in the 60's was backcombed to extinction and piled up in great swathes in a beehive shape. My brother, Norris, once asked if I put chicken wire inside to keep it up. 'I wouldn't be surprised if I didn't find a couple of chickens in there as well,' he grinned. It was impossible to comb out and once sprayed, it stayed like that for a week. Don't ask about sleeping with it!

As I was getting ready my father would invariably say, "Are you going out again? You went out last Saturday." Oh how times have changed.

The boys would often go to a pub before they went to the dance, but the girls would go straight to the ballroom. It was a rarity if you saw a girl in a public house. You would always arrange to meet your partner inside, as boys were expected to pay for everything on a date. Going 'Dutch' was unheard of. Only when you became engaged did you meet outside the hall.

The halls/ballrooms were always packed. Men would stand on one side and the girls on the other. Females would take up their positions, desperately trying to appear dis-interested and wait for those magic words, "May I have this dance?" (And yes they did really did talk like that!) It was shortened as the years sped by to a raised eyebrow and a flick of the head towards the dance floor. Upon reflection, it must have taken a great deal of courage by the lads, who having made the effort to go up to the girl, usually standing the length of the ballroom away, would occasionally get a knock-back with a sniffy, 'no thanks.' Quickly, so as not too lose face, he would ask the girl standing nearby. After three refusals in a row, confidence was completely destroyed and it was an almighty trek back to his place. It often took another two or three dances before he plucked up courage to try again.

David Jason would agree wholeheartedly. He recalls the dance hall days vividly. He likened walking across the floor to ask a girl to dance as "like walking into the mouth of Hell and there was nothing more exasperating than when you'd plucked up the courage and she's accepted, you would move onto the floor only to find that it was the last dance of a three dance sequence and you'd have to start all over again."

David Leith of West Yorkshire recalls the time when he was in a dance hall and he noticed *Alma Cogan,* his favourite singer stood near the entrance. "I thought I'd push my luck and ask her to dance. She smiled as I approached which gave me confidence. 'Will you dance with me?' I asked. 'I'd be delighted,' she replied. I walked onto the floor in a daze which to be honest continued throughout the waltz. She moved perfectly with the rhythm of the music. Miss Cogan was every bit as I'd imagined her to be. Vivacious and charming. It remains one of my most treasured memories."

The late *Harry Secombe* met his wife Myra, at a dance. He said he'd only been demobbed for three days when he decided to go to a local dance hall in Swansea. "It was love at first sight," he revealed. "I was pretending to be a Canadian at the time. I asked her to dance as I imagined a Mountie might do

25

and she looked me straight in the eye and said, ' From Swansea aren't you?' I felt a bloody idiot, but Myra still accepted the dance."

Harry was not on his own in telling girls porkies. I've met film producers, pilots, surgeons and professional footballers - I found the pilot worked on the docks and the film producer was very embarrassed when I found him emptying my dustbin. But the two footballers I dated, were telling the truth. Tommy Forgan and John Savage were both goalkeepers for Hull City. Must be something about goalies, I married one - Oh and he played a saxophone as well!

Many girls, if they didn't get asked or didn't fancy anyone, just danced with each other
I remember at the Regal Ballroom, Beverley, a girl had refused several boys in a row, and **Bert Baker** the MC had seen this and told her if she kept that up she would be barred. He explained: "She'd come to dance, so dance she must."

But sometimes girls would just hang around trying to pretend they didn't care that no-one had asked them to dance. These were known as 'wallflowers'. This reminds me of a story told to me by the late *Kenneth Williams*. It was on his West End debut. "The stage was set as a dance hall and all the girls were sat around in a semi-circle waiting to be asked for a dance. The music started up and at that point pieces of chiffon would come streaming from the ceiling. We ignored the girls and danced with our piece of chiffon. The girls were dressed as wallflowers." He went on: "It was quite sad really, but on the first night, my piece of chiffon never dropped low enough and I spent the whole scene leaping up like a lunatic to catch the end."

There were quite a few military camps in the Hull area and they would arrange dances. Coaches would pick up the local female talent and take them to the camp. Nurses and telephonists were invited en-masse. The most popular camp with all eligible females was undoubtedly the US bases at Driffield and Holme-on-Spalding Moor. They always made sure there was plenty to eat as well as generously dispensing gifts among the impressionable girls. Usually chocolate bars, chewing gum and nylons.
A friend of mine, who tried to wangle a trip every time, told me: "I love them. It's like waking up and finding myself in Heaven."

The dance halls were many and varied. *Roy Wilkin* recalls: "One hall had a stage that was so 'raked' that all the music stands kept creeping forward. It was a nightmare, as my drum kit kept sliding away from me. I was playing most of the night with one hand while hanging desperately onto my cymbals with the other."

Not a lot you can say to that!

George Wilcox chipped in: "The opposite applied to us. One night the band had to perform on individual raised platforms. But the lead trumpet was expected to stand on a sort of column, at least ten feet high all on his own. He was in full flow with a solo and leant back to make that top C, but he leant too far and toppled off the thing. All we heard was a strangled note, followed by aarrgghh!! Without batting an eyelid the band carried on."

Musicians are a race on their own with a vocabulary all to themselves - as I found out. They are also fun people with a wicked sense of humour. I was at a dance when the compere announced over the microphone. "Nobody ever gets up for the first dance, so we'll play the second dance first and the first second. Please take your partners for a quickstep."

Would you believe three couples got up immediately.

As I said, I've chatted to innumerable musicians who regaled me with poignant, funny and interesting stories about an era which sadly will never return. So courtesy of the dance band musicians, we recall those special memories from 'gigs' which are no longer part of the leisure scene.

By the way the term 'gig', is derived from the 16th century 'jig' It was defined as "as a lively piece of music," as is the French "gigue". Also many musicians would try out their latest innovations for a 'giggle,' or as they now say, 'gig'.

Believe me the recollections and gags come thick and fast when a posse of musicians get together. Some, no make that many, are unprintable.

One that springs to mind was told to me on three separate occasions - all by trumpeters! - A young seventeen year old was being lusted after by several band members, but eventually it was a member of the rhythm section who managed to dally with her affections. After one date he couldn't wait to tell the band what had happened. He told them they were stripped and ready for action and his male protuberance was showing signs of excitement. (Not his words, but I'll gloss over that bit!) Anyway, don't forget this was in the days no one spoke of taking precautions. In fact you didn't really speak about it at all. - Just to digress for a minute, I remember seeing a red neon sign outside a chemist, which read Durex. I had no idea what it meant but I knew it was rude, and I couldn't believe it could be put on display like that. I was sixteen! - Anyway back to the young musician and friend. Instead of asking him if he was 'prepared,' she started to tap out the tune 'Button Up Your Overcoat,' on his erect appendage. Well she was a pianist!

Ray DesForges suggested I called the book, 'Nelsons or a Gregory? I realised this was rhyming slang but didn't know for what. He explained: "When a gig is booked, the fee is agreed and a muso. will ask, " Nelsons (short for Nelson Eddy's - readies) or a Gregory (Gregory Peck - cheque)
    I was impressed, but thought, non-musical types like me, wouldn't have a clue what the title meant.

Most of the stories are from the fifties and sixties when drugs were not widely used. One drummer - who asked not to be named - said on his way back from a gig, he found a pill in his pocket, he recognised it as a 'livener' and thought he'd give it a try as he was by now completely whacked after a long session. "An hour later I had no idea what I was doing and had to ring my girlfriend to ask whether I'd already done the show or was I travelling up to it. Needless to say, I made that my one and only dabble with unknown substances."

He was lucky he had a car. In the early days musicians walked, biked or went on the bus. *Roy Wilkin* told me of four musicians who were travelling to a venue on Anlaby Road in Hull. There was a regular trolley-bus service on the route and they all boarded carrying their instruments, a double bass, two trumpets and a tenor sax." Roy said, "They piled them under the stairs and shot up to the top deck for a fag. After the dance they headed for the trolly stop only to find the last one had gone. They tossed for who would go all the way with the bassist as he needed help lugging the thing home. You might know he lived the furthest away!'

He laughed: "I know one story you might like," he said. "We were playing on an out of town gig and decided to hire a van. We arrived at the venue with only twenty minutes to go and we all piled out to get the instruments from the back of the van. John had only locked the keys inside! We couldn't get in the back or front, even with a crowbar. Eventually we did manage to prize open a space large enough for the pianist to squeeze through and he kicked the back doors open from the inside. We got a huge cheer from the punters as we carried our instruments inside. We were only five minutes late."

Someone else who had to make his own way was the bass player *Martin Shaw*. He told me: "I only had a pedal bike, so if I had a gig I would have to put a trailer on the back to carry my double bass. It was a nightmare if it was raining and even worse if there was a wind as well."

It was in the fifties that amplifiers came on the scene. At one dance, the bass player was showing off with his new equipment. He put the controls on loud! The rest of the band complained bitterly, likening it to 'a farting herd of camels with diarrhoea'.

Victor Sylvester was synonymous with ballrooms. He was at his peak during the forties, fifties and sixties.

While researching for this book I found out some interesting facts about Mr Sylvester. He was born on the day Mafeking was relieved, during the Boer war. Hence the name Victor. He enlisted in the army at fourteen and suddenly found himself in Belgium and France before his age became known. He had acquired great skill as a marksman and was assigned to a number of firing squads for the execution of deserters. Years later he realised the enormity of his actions and experienced deep regret for them.

Victor Junior joined the band in 1945 as a booking manager but took over as leader in 1971 and performed until 1998, a year before he died.

In those days it was inconceivable you could dance to records, but we reckoned without *Jimmy Saville*.

He started his career as assistant manager at the Locarno Ballroom in Leeds, which was documented as pulling in over a thousand punters a night.

It was Jimmy's proud boast that he invented the twin turntable while he was at Leeds. He said, "It took me ten years to persuade the punters that dancing to records was okay. Leeds was the first place in the world to organise disco's."

Organisers soon realised one man spinning discs was infinitely more profitable that paying a band, however small and so the erosion began.

Bert Boots, a well-known local bass player, immigrated to Australia just as ballrooms were becoming obsolete. "But," he said, "they were non-existent over there and I missed the music scene a great deal."

He recalled the time when he'd taken his wife Kay out to a local restaurant in Perth for a celebration meal. A piano was being played softly in the background and Bert decided he'd like to meet the pianist, as he was obviously a highly accomplished musician and it was so unusual to hear 'live' music.

"I couldn't see a piano, so I asked the waiter where he was. He pointed to a black box on the edge of the bar, a sort of modern piano. Seeing that lump of plastic sat there ruined the whole evening," said Bert, "it had no heart or soul."

He asked the manager why he didn't get a 'real' pianist, as it would add ambience to otherwise excellent restaurant.

"You've got to be joking," was the reply. That black box doesn't cost me any money and it sure as hell doesn't drink as much."

Instruments cost a great deal of money and musicians often suffered hardship to obtain their dream. Nearly all were second-hand and on the never-never. Piano's were the exception but in the twenty-first century this is no longer the case. Now keyboard players take their electronic instrument along to the gig. Piano's cost a veritable fortune and anyway stages are so small they cannot be accommodated in this modern world. I did read about a new piano on the market. It costs two hundred and ten THOUSAND pounds! It's controlled by a computer chip, now there's a surprise, and it takes seven months to make. It features voice activation, a touch screen monitor and many other gadgets. It has the moniker of 'The Disklaver Pro 2000.' It said in the blurb it's built around a Pentium 111 computer chip.

And that's music?!

Recently I went to a party where a live band had been booked. I spoke to several teenagers, who asked, "Are they really playing those instruments?"

At the same party a young man approached the hostess and said he was enjoying the night and added, "But I am surprised they haven't got a plank spanker with them."

The hostess was puzzled, but didn't let on to the youth she hadn't a clue what he was talking about and as soon as there was a lull asked the band leader: "What the hell is a plank spanker?" He laughed and said "It comes from the states and is the latest speak for a guitar player."

Wow, what a relief!

Oh, by the way before I forget. Do you know who was presented with the first ever Gold Disc? To give you a clue it was in February 1942.

The song was Chattanooga Choo Choo and the artist was *Glen Miller.*

This was a time when the top ten was determined by the sales of sheet music.

While interviewing musicians for this book I met **Norman Baron.** Norman hailed from Southend and came to Hull with the *Ivor Kirchin Band* who opened the Locarno Ballroom and like many others decided to stay.

Norman confided that he'd wanted to write about his many experiences travelling on the Mecca circuit with the big band. "I made notes, daily and fully intended getting it typed up," he told me. "Then I suddenly realised how explosive the material was. All the stories were either against the law or against the vows of marriage. All my friends would have been arrested or divorced within six months of being published. Afraid I couldn't live with that on my conscience."

But Norman did tell me a quite few repeatable stories and I know you'll love them.

He had played for many years in London and recalls chatting casually to a fellow trumpet player, in some high rise flats. "Suddenly he went out onto the balcony and literally stepped into the night. Seventeen floors up! I hope he wasn't making a comment on my trumpet playing.

Again in London I'd just finished a gig in a hotel and was making my way to my car, when a lady of the night approached me and asked 'if I'd like a good

31

time.' I explained I'd also been working all night an just wanted to get home and anyway I only had enough money for a gallon of petrol. 'Well will you do me a favour then?' she asked, 'can you drive me to the front of the hotel and drop me off, that way they'll think I'm a guest.' I did as I was asked and as she was getting out of the car she turned and said, 'you've been so kind, how about twenty-five pounds?' I explained again I only had a couple of quid on me, 'That's all right,' she said, "I take Mastercard and American Express!"

He also brought to mind the time the band was playing under a marquee for a wedding party. "The guests were mingling on the lawn waiting for the bride and groom to return from the church. The wind had been a problem all afternoon, when suddenly a particularly vicious gust, whisked the whole marquee over on its side. The band never missed a note, even though our music was being spread in great abandonment all over the area. Guests were rushing around picking the sheets up and one guest tidied them all up together and as he handed them to the band leader, he asked if he wanted him to put them back on the stands. He was delighted. 'obviously a musician,' he thought, and nodded enthusiastically. The guy carefully placed several sheets on each stand. Problem: Trumpets were mixed with keyboards, bass with trombones etc. When the 'helpful' guest saw them being handed en masse to the keyboard player, he came across and asked what was wrong. When it was explained all the musicians had different music, he looked astounded and said, "They don't do they?"

"But the problems didn't stop there," said Norman, "Later, we were inside the building playing for the reception, when the time came to cut the four tiered cake. The drummer gave a roll on the drums, to great effect, but as the knife was pressed into the bottom layer, it suddenly tipped over and smashed onto the floor. The guests were rolling about in hysterical laughter, when to make things worse, the bride's mother rushed forward, slipped on the cake and crashed to the ground. The father tried to pick her up but landed on a heap on top of her.

"This all happened before video recorders," said Norman, "or it would have given enough material for a whole programme of 'Have You Been Framed'."

He also recalled the time a six-piece arrived at the venue to find no piano. The bandleader went to tackle the manager.

"Where's the bloody piano?"

" Sorry," he told him, " I didn't think you'd need one."

Don't forget electronic keyboards hadn't even been invented then.

We eventually borrowed one from a nearby pub, luckily it had wheels, but we were an hour late going on the stand. It took ten people just to get the monstrosity into the place. I don't know why we bothered. The bloody thing was so out of tune it sounded like a fairground ride. We had a female singer who refused point blank after the first number to do another song. I wouldn't mind but none of the punters noticed. They told us they'd had a wonderful night and booked us for the next year."

He groaned. "Oh God, that reminds me of another piano story. For a while I ran a band called *Jazz Machine* and once we arrived at a gig and found the bloody piano twenty yards away from the stage. We were heaving the thing into position when it got caught in the carpet and toppled over. *Fred Yeadon*, the pianist, started to play and found it was a semi-tone out so spent the entire night transposing the dots as he played."

But I think my favourite story from Norman concerned a young man who had collapsed on the dance floor. "They called an ambulance and the girl he'd been dancing with told us, ' one minute he was dancing and the next minute he collapsed unconscious on the floor.' He was turning blue before our eyes. I've never seen anything like it. The ambulance drivers were convinced he'd had a heart attack and quickly loaded him into the ambulance.

"We heard later that he died on his way to hospital." Norman gave me a cheeky grin and leant forward. "And this is God's honest truth. They were checking the cause of death and when the nurses removed his clothes, they found he'd strapped a roll of material to his crotch to make his 'personal attributes' appear larger. Unfortunately he'd tied it with surgical tubing which had cut off the circulation to his leg. Apparently the blood flow, combined with the exertion of dancing, triggered the heart attack."

As I told Norman, "You see size does matter - if his brain had been larger, he'd still be alive today."

I had made arrangements to chat to him again with his friend *Donny Keith*, vocalist with the *Ivor Kirchin Band*, when Norman suddenly contracted Leukaemia and sadly died.

Musicians came from far and wide to the funeral. Everyone had wonderful memories of a more than competent trumpeter and an all-round nice guy. So I made a vow then to finish the book and hopefully convey the great fun experienced by musicians far and wide. Not a disgraceful anecdote in sight - well not many!

I hope Norman approves.

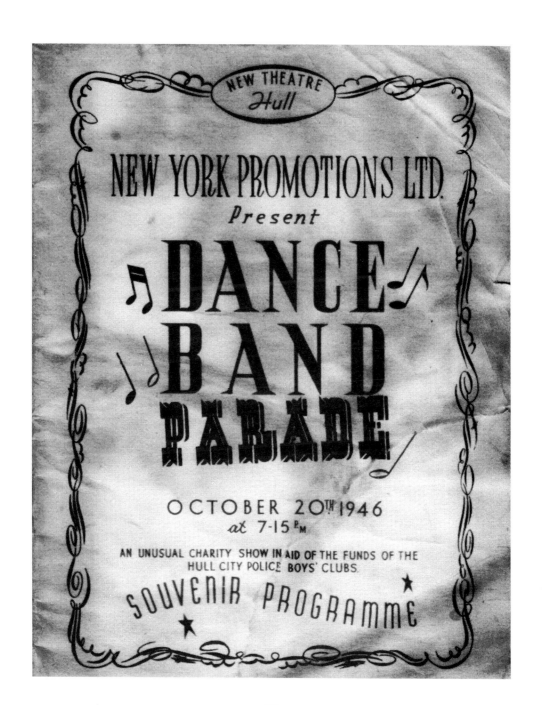

WHITE HOUSE
HOTEL

NOW OPEN FOR RESIDENTS

DANCE

NEW YORK

In Aid of the Funds

PRO

PART ONE

1. **HAROLD DAWSON and his NEW YORKERS.**
    (*Introduced by their signature tune*—"You and the Night and the Music").

    (*a*) POLLY WOLLY DOODLE.

    (*b*) DANNY BOY—Featuring "THE BRASS BELLS."

    (*c*) DRINK TO ME ONLY.

    (*d*) ANVIL CHORUS.

2. **THE WHITE HOUSE SWINGTETTE, directed by Arthur Gibbins.**

    (*a*) SLIPPED DISC.

    (*b*) SUMMERTIME.

    (*c*) FRONT AND CENTER.

3. **GUEST ARTISTE** - - - **RON PARRY**

    "Design for Laughter."

4. **HAROLD DAWSON and his NEW YORKERS.**

    (*a*) TAMPICO.

    (*b*) SKYLINER.

In

The Show Compered by Ll

D PARADE

THE HOUSE OF MIRELL

For Autumn Elegance

OTIONS LTD

City Police Boys' Clubs.

MME

PART TWO

5. **HAROLD DAWSON and his NEW YORKERS.**
   - (a) MY BABY SAID YES.
   - (b) SONG OF THE VOLGA BOATMEN.
   - (c) PICK A RIB.

6. **THE BLUE HAWAIIANS and THE DIXIELANDERS.**

(a) PALIKIKO BLUES.	(b) AT THE JAZZ BAND BALL.
(c) SONG OF THE ISLANDS.	(d) DIPPERMOUTH BLUES

7. **THE PIANISTICS (Gibbins and Stewart).**
   - (a) SKATERS WALTZ.
   - (b) CLAIR DE LUNE.

7. **GUEST ARTISTES** - - - **"THE TWO GAY BACHELORS"**

   B.B.C. and West End Cabaret Stars.

8. **HAROLD DAWSON and his NEW YORKERS.**
   - (a) JINGLE BELLS.
   - (b) LAUGHING ON THE OUTSIDE.
   - (c) MEXICAN HAT DANCE.

inutes

MS *B.B.C. Dance Band Announcer*

THE START OF SOMETHING BIG

Many musicians learnt their craft in the 'Student Orchestra' a weekly session run by experienced musicians giving them a wonderful opportunity to experience working in a band environment and of course bandleaders the chance to spot new talent.

The Musicians Union said: "One of the conditions of joining the orchestra is that students must become members of the Union and in this improvement of their musicianship brings with it improvement of their understanding of the need to strengthen the union."

The Hull Daily Mail showed a great interest in this project and ran a double page spread on the venture.

HULL DAILY MAIL FEBRUARY 5th 1954

'They CAN Tell A Waltz From A Tango.'

Sweet music and trade unionism walks hand in hand to the Windsor Hall, Anlaby Road, every Sunday morning when more than 30 young people join together under experienced musicians to produce high notes, low notes and blue notes - in fact, to play dance music.

But the 32 young men and a girl seldom wear evening clothes, and only critical professionals ever hear the orchestra, for every one of the instrumentalist is learning the strict tempo business with an eye to joining a dance band. Some already have places in local bands, but they continue to go to this unusual "Sunday school." for in a competitive world mere proficiency is not enough.

The venture is backed by Hull branch of the Musician's Union and everyone who joins the class - even a 15-year-old schoolgirl (*Yvonne Bailey*) must also join the union. And the union sees to it that they are trained well enough to justify the hypothetical payments they may receive in the future.

Playing popular music is a competitive business and the difficulties the youngsters face in starting off are smoothed out by the union's musical guides.

One of them, *Teddy Barker*, forced into a successful musical career by two accidents, spends most nights writing the special orchestrations for this unusual orchestra which will never play in public.

Hull is the only Musicians' Union branch to put the policy into practise, but the idea has proved such a great success that other branches may follow.

Chief instructors, along with Teddy Barker, are *Bert Brooks* (secretary) *Roy Longbottom*, both saxophone experts: *Tommy Sykes*, trumpet: *Don Washbrook*, Trombone: and *Pat Cornell*, drums.

They are out to break the vicious circle in which dance orchestras refuse to employ inexperienced players who to get experience must play with an orchestra.

Into the tiny hall each Sunday march 10 saxophones, five trumpets, four trombones, a rhythm section - consisting of piano, drums, guitar - and a double bass with a man underneath.

This latter is played by a salesman, *Leslie Jordan*. At 22 he already knows enough about the trombone and allied instruments to play in a yeomanry band.

Unabashed by the attention of neighbours - for the double bass can sound very lonely playing scales and that of children who chase behind him in the street, he hauls his instrument on to his back and staggers from his home in St. Georges Rd. to join the rest for practise.

As they assemble, these young players join their appropriate group for the morning's work. At the end of the section practise, they return to the main hall, where less advanced students have been practising, and the whole crowds then form the great orchestra.

It is during this last half-hour that the most valuable experience of all is gained, and the most concentration of effort is made.

Ray Scott (21) of Margaret St. Beverley Rd., worked overtime as a gas fitter to buy a new alto sax costing £60. Now he must go into the forces for two years, but like most of those called up, he will take his sax with him and look for a place in the nearest band.

SAX'S: *Ray DesForges, Ray Scott. Roy Green, John Grindley, Norman Corner, Dave Ramsden, John Proctor, Everard Snowdon, Joe Cleveland, Mike Irwin,*

TRUMPETS; *George Moffat , Jack Vincent, Pete Dawson,*

DRUMS: *Ken Ormston, Griff Williams, Barrie Hilton, Peter Morley, Roy Wilkin*

PIANO; *Yvonne Bailey*

BASS: *Les Jordan*

TROMBONES: *John Hardy, Phil*

By the way all the musicians I spoke to remembered with affection the 'student' days.

And all remembered Miss Bailey, especially her lovely complexion,' said one. Oh yes!!

Student Orchestra fronted by Eddie Gray, Skyline Ballroom, Hull

Wold Road School, 1956. Back: Roy
Wilkin - Front: Graham Joy

Wold Road School, 1956. L/R: Dave
Cottam, Ray Desforges, John Grindley

Musician Union's Dinner. L/R: Griff Williams, Mrs Williams, Bert Hickey, Wynn Hickey, Sheila Edkins, Tom Glenton

Wold Road School 1956. Ray Desforges

Pete Dawson with Friend, 1956

Lawson-Taylor Entertainments

NEWINGTON HALL

For BETTER DANCING!

MODERN TONIGHT
8 to 12.   3/-.
Newington Orchestra.

SATURDAY, 7.30 to 11.30. 3/-
HARRY CHATTERTON
and his Modernaires
with "The Crackajacks."
Also **MONDAY**, 8 to 11.   2/-.

CITY HALL

"All Roads Lead There"
SATURDAY, 7.30 to 11.30. 4/-
NEWINGTON ORCHESTRA
with vocals by **Don Holden,**
George Cox and **The Blue**
Notes.
M.C.s: Harry Brandon & Staff.
Grange Catering. Late Buses.

L/R Len Rangely, Pete Mimms, Norman Baron, Andy Peacock, Baz Hewland, Gary Gillyett

BANDS FROM THE SWINGING YEARS

TEDDY BARKER

Teddy played piano and was resident with his band at the New York Hotel. 'Teddy Barker's Modern Music group.' His vocalist **Wynn Hickey** told me, "In December, 1955, **Pete Wainwright** who played bass with him, went to London to become a professional musician. But he had a phobia," confessed Wynn. "He do almost anything to avoid having his photograph taken. In fact the Hull Times ran a story about him he point blank refused to have his picture taken for the article."

Teddy was also renowned for playing loudly, VERY loudly. The diners would try to talk over the music, "and," said Wynn, "I couldn't count the times, they were still shouting their heads off and we'd stopped playing. They were always so embarrassed."

To record some jazz, Teddy brought in some recognised jazz players. **Ron Dunne** on drums, **Gerry Rollinson**, vibes and **Noel Flint**, bass. They recorded a gig at the Hull University. They made a limited edition of twenty discs.

Teddy also wrote music. One speciality was 'The New York Suite.' This was recorded on a Sunday afternoon at the New York Hotel. It's thought Kay Garner sang on that recording.

Some more names who played with Teddy:
Bass: **John Carnazza,**
Tenor: **Roy Longbottom**
Guitar: **Vic Cheeseman**
Drums: **Ray Aldridge**

JACK BARKER

"His band was a delight to play in," said *Alf Stephenson*, "Every member had a sense of humour and they all helped out the youngsters who came in. I bought my first American trumpet when I played for him, it cost £157. Everybody wanted one, but they had an import ban for many years."

Brian Hargrave remembers a musician, "Who shall be nameless," said Brian, "who managed to imbibe eight brandies and rums in the interval. He came back half-an-hour late and played the rest of the night half-a-beat behind the drummer."

Trevor Hickson recalls Jack as, "a lovely player. Especially jazz."

BLUE RHYTHM SWINGTETTE

Personnel included, *Roy Wilkie - Dave Cottam - John Grindley - Pete Dawson - and Ray DesForges*. Formed in the 50's, they played mainly in church halls and Wold Road School. Roy Wilkin recalls the time they were playing in a church hall and there was a sash window at the back of the stage. "This proved very useful," said Roy, "because I opened the window and used the sill as my seat. I had to perch there all night. Very uncomfortable. But we all enjoyed it."

Most of them soon joined larger bands in the area, but as *John Grindley* said, "It was great experience for us."

ALAN BOND (Bert Boots)

In the late 40's he formed a band to open up the refurbished Jackson's Ballroom.

Personnel included: Drums: *Bert Hickey* - Bass: *Bert Boots* - Keyboard: *Bob Grant*.

Saxes: *Gerry Shakespeare, Norman Horsefall* and *Colin Shakespeare*.

Trumpets: *Tom Glenton*.

Vocalists: *Wynn Hickey* and *Ken Tuson*.

"I originally played the alto sax, said Bert Boots, "I wish I'd stayed with it. Have you ever tried boarding a bus with a string bass? Musicians with cars often helped me out, otherwise I'd strap it to my back and cycle to gigs. Although," said Bert, " my progress was almost entirely dependent on the direction of the wind."

"How did you come by your first bass?" I asked

"When the Tivoli Theatre in Hull, closed the musician who played in the pit decided to retire and sold his bass to the Paragon Music Stores. I bought it for the princely sum of twelve pounds. Many years later I sold it to the bass player of the ABC Symphony Orchestra in Perth, Australia for $100. I've heard it's worth five times that now."

Bert said he'd heard that when **Monty Sunshine** started a band they'd found an old coal merchant's lorry for sale. "Then one of the boys said he knew where they could get the back of an ambulance. So they put one on top of the other. Evidently on their first run out, they'd equipped it with a couple of armchairs and a deckchair. They went round the first corner and wallop, the lot ended up on the floor. Still, had to be better than my bike," said Bert.

"When I came back to Hull, I played at the many forces camps throughout the area. At RAF Sutton-On-Hull I was joined by **Frank Harrison** on piano.
Wrestling matches were a popular form of entertainment in Sutton and as the stage was above the ring, the musicians got a grandstand view.

"We used to get a free supper, mainly, because they seldom paid us. At one dance, held in the officer's mess, there was an un-ending supply of free drinks and true to all musicians, we were imbibing freely. At the time I was playing second alto and was situated in the centre of the line up. I tentatively attempted to stand upright and found that the boys either side were using me as a stabilising force to stay erect."

Bert smiled as he recalled the time they were all sitting in the back of a truck on the way to a gig. "Suddenly the pianist jumped over the tailgate onto the road. With horror we saw him turn a few somersaults then disappear from view as we rounded a bend. Much yelling and banging and the driver came to a standstill. We all rushed out, expecting the worst when suddenly he came sauntering towards us, completely unconcerned. 'What the hell were you doing? We asked. 'I couldn't stand the bloody exhaust fumes, so I got out before you had a dead piano player. ' He was allowed to ride with the driver. I thought afterwards what a crafty so-and-so, I wish I'd thought of it."

He continued. "I had a super vocalist at those camp dances *Joan Richardson*) (Jo. Peters). She went on to become professional."

"It was perfect experience for the big time." Joanne took up the story. "I remember the time when we'd finished a gig and were boarding the transport to return home. As usual one of the trumpet players was missing. We knew he'd be offering his favours to a girl, so hung around for about half-an-hour.

"Sod him," said a band member, "I've to be at work at seven."

"We all felt very guilty but went without him. When we saw him next, he told us. 'Hey, lads I struck it bloody lucky the other night."

"We guessed that," we said.

"No, I mean she borrowed her dad's car to take me home. I was in Hull by one."

"You got hung for murder in those days," said Joanne, " but rolled up dots made a pretty fair substitute to get even."

"When I went down to London to try my luck. I met *Barney Colehan* who was my mentor. He used to arrange auditions for me. I eventually travelled the country singing with some of the leading dance bands of the day including *Geraldo* and the *Joe Loss Orchestra*. Joe Loss always called me Yossel, which is the Jewish name for Joe. Mainly because when somebody shouted Jo, we'd both answer. Even the band called me Yossel. I was the only girl with probably fifteen/ sixteen guys and they all looked after me. No one could try and ogle me without having to pass muster with 'my uncles' first. I remember one occasion when a young man was getting quite persistent and he was stood at the front of the stage. One of the trombonists got up to do a solo and he put his slide out as far as it would go, just to frighten him off, except the thing shot off and nearly de-capitated the poor man. It did the trick though, I never saw him again."

Joanne said the boys weren't supposed to drink before a gig, so many of them would top up a coke bottle with their favourite tipple and swig innocently from that.

She retired in the early sixties, but carried for many years giving outstanding performances on the amateur stage in such memorable productions as Hello Dolly, Cabaret and The King and I.

Bert Boots said he also played for many years with *Harry Chatterton* and *Bill Kinsey*, before emigrating to Australia, where he still keeps in touch with his many friends.

MIKE BROWN & HIS ORCHESTRA

Although this band wasn't formed until 1999/2000, I feel it's important to include it as so many of the musicians playing, were regulars in the bands from the 'dancing years.'

Mike, a music teacher, is an accomplished arranger with many of his orchestrations accepted by the B.B.C Big Band.

The orchestra gigs around but also plays strictly for dancing once a month at the Walton Street Club in Hull.

It's a tight, well rehearsed sound, bringing back the punch and verve of the big band sound.'

(And Mike didn't have one naughty story to tell me, but I'd had so many from most of the band I let him off).

Line-up includes: *Mike Brown* (leader/arranger/trumpet/flugel)

Saxes: *George Wilcox, Ralph Alder, John Mallinder, Len Rangely, Noel Weston, Julie Alder, Rachel Hammerton.*

Trumpets: *Keith Parker, Alf Stephenson, Brian Hargrave, Dixon Laing, Gemma Reed* and *Rachel Collinson.*

Trombones: *Pete Reed, Stuart Wilkinson, Rebecca Bull, Caroline Shepherd, Nick Garside, Dave Haworth, Roy Cooper.*

Keyboard: *Dave Deighton, Rob Barron.*

Drums: *Pete Parker.*

Bass: *Paul Gibbins.*

Vocals: *Jim Lundy, Emily Butterfield, Brenda Fountain.*

CECIL THEATRE BAND

(The Cecil Theatre was owned by Brindley Evans.)
    Personnel: Vocalist: *Wynn Hickey*. Trumpet: *Maxwell Daniels*; Violin: *Wally Tuson*

It re-opened 1955 with a regular band plus one of those wonderful organs, which rose from the depths of the building to play for the patrons before the big picture started.

Wynn recalls, "We used to rehearse in the afternoons, so that meant having to walk to the cinema with my baby son Andrew in a pram. It must have had an effect on him as he went to Music College and is now a professional musician working in Manchester.

We were playing to full houses nearly all the time. I remember one night the violinist, *Wally Tuson*, felt sick, so he took out his palette, with two false teeth attached. I was sat nearby so he handed them to me. 'I don't want them', I told him, and pushed them back on his lap. He leaned backwards and popped them on the top of the radiator, but they fell down the back. At the end of the night we all had a go at retrieving them but to no avail. They're probably still there," said Wynn.

HARRY CHATTERTON

Where do I start? Every musician I spoke to held Harry in the highest regard. He was recognised as a superb trombone player by top professional players throughout Britain.

Don Lusher was a personal friend and at a gig at Hull university with *Kenny Baker*, - who played for Harry at the Withernsea Pavilion - he told the audience about Harry's prowess with a trombone. "The first time I heard him play was with the Squadronairres and he made my hair stand on end." He then went on to dedicate the next number 'Stardust,' to Harry.

High praise indeed.

Harry's wife Doreen ferried him around to the gigs, dropping him off at the venue and returning later to pick him up. "Didn't he drive?" I asked. "Oh, yes, but only a little blue invalid car, which wasn't really suitable."

She told me he played for quite a time with the Hessle Brass Band: "We'd all gone to the Royal Albert Hall in London for a competition. In the evening, we decided to go to the 101 Club in Oxford Street. The rest of the band asked what we were doing and Harry told them. Several wanted to come but Harry told them they wouldn't like it as it was jazz, but undeterred, about twelve said they wanted to give it a try. While we were at the club *Dixon Laing*, our trumpet player, kept pestering the band leader to let Harry have a go. He wasn't impressed, but Dixon became so insistent, he eventually said okay. 'Where are you from?' he asked. Hull, they told him. 'Oh, that fishing village up north. And what band are you with? His face was a picture when they told him we were brass band players." She smiled, "and it certainly didn't help his initial conviction that we were out-of-town-hicks when Harry made his way to the stage supported by two sticks. The lads physically lifted him onto the stage, where first he put his sticks on the top of the piano and he was then handed the trombone. 'How do you play this thing?' he asked the musician and proceeded to oil the slide. The bandleader then announced: 'ladies and gentlemen this is that fish town player.' Then Harry started to play. The place erupted. The pro. was rendered speechless. Suffice to say he was an immediate hit. As he came off stage he was approached by an agent who offered him a two-year contract, but he wasn't interested. The owner of the club was so impressed he offered Harry and me life membership."

Doreen told me she'd gone to London a few years after Harry's death, "and do you know they still remembered him."

She also recalled a concert at the Hull City Hall, "as an extra to the Hull Philharmonic, with *Geoffrey Heald-Smith* as conductor. The classical orchestra trooped off and Harry came on to try and show them what jazz was all about. The audience loved it. Mind you I suppose it helped having Geoffrey on piano and his wife Janet on bass.

The rest of the line-up consisted of *Trevor Hardy* on clarinet and *Martin Beadle* on drums."

Dixon Laing said: "I first met Harry when I was fifteen years old. We were playing in a marquee in the middle of a field and the whole place was littered in cow pats. There was only half-a-dozen people in there. As soon as we'd

51

finished the first set we all headed to the beer tent. I was stood next to Harry and I asked why he was playing out of his skin when nobody was listening. Harry looked directly into my eyes, 'I'm listening son,' he said. I've never forgotten that."

This comment reminded *Eric Wright* of the time he was playing with Chat. "We had *Trevor Hickson, Alan Harmer, Freddie Harrison* and *Dave Peacock* was on banjo. Suddenly Dave stopped playing and later Chat. told him, 'Don't ever stop playing son. It doesn't matter what happens, keep going 'till it sorts itself out - Good advice," said Eric.

A little story about *Dave Peacock. Trevor Hickson* told me they were playing at Cleethorpes and Dave was constantly muttering about being cold. "It turned out he'd only been sitting on the bingo prize - a joint of frozen beef!"

Dixon has a sound background in the brass band world having played with Grimethorpe Colliery and travelled Europe with the renowned Black Dyke Colliery Band.

"Harry asked me to play trumpet for him but I'd only played cornet, so borrowed my nephews. We had a gig at the New Theatre and it was a show called The Waltz Dream. I wish I'd had a disguise to get out of the theatre. I was completely out of my depth. But Harry persevered with me.

At the time I worked 6am to 2pm at Birds Eye and earned £12 a week. At the end of my stint at the theatre Harry presented me with £24. I thought Christmas had come early.

Harry then decided to form a dance band called the Brass Hats with only brass band players. To prove a point really. We had *Mike Frederick* and *Harry Anderson* on trumpets.

John Jefferson and *Harry Chatterton* on trombones, *Fred Harrison* bass guitar, somebody *Naylor* was on drums and *Malcolm Allsop* was lead guitar."

I was told Harry often used to pinch arrangements from a band called 'Ray Davies and his Button Down Brass.' "They were really top notch and the arrangements were spot on."

Dixon also recalled the time they'd all gone to a music trade fair. *John Pollard*, the top trombonist from from Grimethorpe Colliery Band was at a stand trying out an instrument. An admiring crowd surrounded him. We were just looking at mouthpieces when Harry picked up a trombone. Can I try it? He asked, 'of course,' was the reply. Harry lifted it up to his lip and tore off the most amazing hot jazz piece I've ever heard. Poor old Pollard wondered where all the crowd had gone."

Harry became almost a legend among the dance fraternity. He was resident in the late 40's at the Fulford Ballroom (latterly the New Brunswick), then in the 50's at the Regal Ballroom, Beverley, until the residency was taken over by the *Bill Kinsey Band.* Later he was resident at the Majestic Ballroom, Witham, with the vocalist *Kay Buliegh*, who later changed her name to Kay Garner and became a session singer in London.

He played on several occasions with the BBC with **J**oan Richardson (Peters) on vocals.

The BBC wanted to audition Joanne and asked her to go to Leeds. Playing the piano was *Violet Carson*, later to become the infamous *Ena Sharples* of Coronation Street. Auditioning the same time as Jo. was another vocalist from Hull, *Adrian Hill*, later to become the very successful *Ronnie Hilton*. Harry eventually left Hull to take a residency in London as a trombonist with the renowned *Cyril Stapleton's Orchestra.*

A bass player told me: "Harry was famed for playing exceptionally long sets. One night during the interval, all had imbibed freely at the bar and in the second half, none of the musicians could manage a full set, so one by one we would sneak outside to relieve ourselves. Later we found out that we were next door to Securicor and our nocturnal habits were on camera!"

Harry was also well known for his dry off the cuff remarks, which often had the musicians in stitches. "I was lucky," said *Paul Gibbins*, "playing bass while giggling is not quite as difficult as the brass section." He went on to tell me: "After a few beers, punters often approached the band and ask if they could sing with them. "For some reason we were never approached by females," said Paul, "well not to sing anyway!"

"Good job, the fellah's were bad enough," said **Bert Boots**. "I remember one night at the City Hall. As soon as this punter started singing we knew he was hopeless and **Frank Harrison**, the pianist started to giggle, which set off the rest of the band. Like Paul said, laughter and wind instruments don't mix. They were all in a heap, leaving the drummer and me on bass, to supplement whatever Frank managed to accomplish between giggles. Now we noticed the dancers were congregating in front of the stage and joining in the fun. The man eventually got the message and slunk off."

"I remember one of the trumpet players had a small plate with three teeth on it," said **Ray Scott**. "It somehow dropped on the floor and a trombone player stood on it. It wouldn't fit back in his mouth. Have you ever heard of a trumpet player with no teeth? Cracked notes filled the air, while the entire band had hysterics. But I wont embarrass him by naming him," said Ray.

"By the way, did you know Harry was famous for something other than playing?"

"No," I enthused, "tell me more".

"He had a false front tooth you know."

"Oh is that all." My pen was put down.

"No listen, it used to be very funny. The bloody thing would never stay in place. He used to carry some type of super glue in his case. We'd see him fiddling around on the floor, looking for the tooth, then he'd forage around in his bag, pick out the tube of glue, cover the offending tooth and pop it back in. But it never worked. Within half-an-hour the bloody thing was rolling around the floor again."

"I don't wonder," said **Dixon Laing**, "because he had the funniest embouchure I've ever seen. He used to push the mouthpiece under his lip. Oh and another thing," said Dixon, "He's the only musician I've ever known that never warmed up."

Eric Wright said they were doing a gig at the Shire Hall, Howden. "As soon as were setting up we noticed an icy blast coming from the back of the stage. We found a broken window, so Harry had an idea. 'Grab the piano cover lads,' he told us. We heaved it to the back and proceeded to block up the offending gap. Left it there too." He laughed. "This was about the time groups were coming on the scene with their loudspeakers. One youth asked Harry how much cable he had to use. Nothing much,' replied Harry. The young man swaggered and told him proudly 'we have more than forty foot. Harry kept commenting on this over the microphone. 'Do you know the next band has over forty-foot of cable. They had no idea he was taking the mickey."

Eric also told me: "Like many bandleaders he put out more than one band, especially at times like New Year's Eve when musicians were at a premium. I'd turned up at Darley's Hotel with *Bill Edkins*, we were at the wrong place it should have been the Goodfellowship on Cottingham Road. We just made it in time and were sorting out the stands when we heard a commotion at the entrance. *Tom Allanson* was being refused entry because he hadn't a ticket, they wouldn't believe he was a musician."

Frank Cleveland recalls the time a punter was being particularly objectionable, so as he was dancing past the stand, Harry casually bopped him on the back of his head, with the slide. The punter whirled around but by then Harry was already pointing the other way with slide raised heavenwards."

"I was once playing with Chat," said *Trevor Hickson*, "and *Frank Harrison* was on the piano. It was a grand. In the interval, as usual, I'd had a few, so when I returned to the stand I told Frank, 'For God's sake don't put that lid down, I need it to lean on."

Paul Shepherdson said they used to play in a club which also had a grand piano. "Trouble was said Paul. They never closed the lid and when it rained it used to drip into the piano. Can you imagine what it sounded like. Anyway it eventually ruined it."

"We were rehearsing with Chat. for the Musician Union's Ball," said *Eric Wright*, and we'd all spent some time carefully putting the dots in order, but at the start we found out Harry had mixed his up, then would you believe, *Trevor Hickson* dropped his pad. He picked the sheets from the floor and quickly replaced them on the stand. To the great consternation of *George Moffat*, he played the whole of the next number with the music upside down."

John Ward remembers the first time he heard Harry's band play 'Peanut vendor.'

"It was at the Fulford and I simply froze on the spot. I'd never heard anything like it before. It was absolute magic."

John, said he sometimes played in a quartet of Harry's. "I originally took lessons from him at a charge of 5/-, with a tot of rum proffered by his mum as an extra incentive." John continued: "In rehearsal, when Harry wanted to stop the band he would put his thumb and forefinger in his mouth and whistle. It just blasted out. It stopped us all in our tracks."

"At one dance at the Beverley Regal, we were backing **Chris Barber's Band**. **Lonny Donegan** was supposed to be on banjo but he felt so ill he was doubled up at the back most of the night. **Kenny Ball** was also on the bill. Anyway during the interval **Trevor Hickson** and I (**Eric Wright**) took them back to sample some of 'Nellies' special at the White Horse. The guest muso's were not impressed, telling us they didn't think the brew was very strong."

Trevor Hickson continued: "When we got outside, they couldn't stand. *Chris Barber* was not impressed!"

"Oh, another thing," said Eric. "Harry had just got a new trombone and was showing it to Chris, who condescendingly showed him how a trombone should be played. Obviously under the impression he was among a load of hicks. Harry got up and literally blew **Chris Barber** off the stage. We were bloody delighted, because we knew Harry was a bloody great musician."

John Carnazza said when he played with Chat. Ivanhoe was popular on the television. "It had a really distinctive introduction and often during the night Chat. would suddenly blast out the recognisable music and everybody would yell 'Ivanhoe!' Great fun and great memories."

A final word from a regular in his band. "When we arrived at a venue, which was serving food, Harry was soon sampling the wares, in fact one night at Driffield Town Hall, they'd arranged a special cake as a prize to be presented later in the evening. Too late Harry had scoffed most of it in the interval. He also was not averse to popping a few, ham rolls, cakes and biscuits in his trombone case to take home."

Some of the musicians who played in the band included:
Piano: *Gordon Findlay.* Drums: *Don Murray.* Bass: *John Carnazza*
Saxes: *Colin Shakespeare*, tenor. *Gordon Roberts*, alto.
Trumpets: *Trevor Hickson, Dennis Whitehead* and *Ernie Watson* who went on to become a highly efficient musician with the BBC Dance Orchestra.
Trombone: *Harry Chatterton.*
His vocalist *Leon Riley*, also went on to have a successful professional career.

FRANK CLEVELAND

His first gig was at the old Danse-de-Luxe on Anlaby Road. He then went on to play with the famous *Sid Phillips*, who had *Kenny Ball* on trumpet.

He recalls the time he was asked to play with *Jack Payne* on second alto. "I was offered £27.10 a week At the time I was earning £12.00 a week, so this was big time. I hesitated and Jack Payne said, 'oh all right then, £35.00.' I think I was too taken aback to say anything but he thought I was stalling, so upped the odds. 'Right, I'll include all expenses.' I casually answered okay then. I thought that was a fortune but I found out that Kenny Ball was on £70 a week, but even then whenever we had to stay over he would book the cheapest digs imaginable. Usually a loft with only a sleeping bag on the floor."

He continued, "Of course in those days, the musician was king. Most of the instruments were given by the manufacturers, they would have a fleet of cars waiting to ferry them around and when they left a town, thousands would turn out to see them go."

During the rock and roll era, Frank ran a small band playing mainly in the Bridlington area. Later joining *Harry Chatterton* at the Newington and latterly at the Brunswick on Beverley Road.

Frank talked animatedly about those halcyon days. Fond recollections of individuals came thick and fast, among them *Johnny Leng*, a keyboard player, who was always seen smoking a long curved pipe. "He was some pianist," said Frank, "and would go on forever. We used to shout, 'get the brakes on Johnny.' There was also *Bernard Alton* who would casually stroll into a dance hall, invariable carrying his clarinet case desperately hoping someone would offer him a gig.

In 1962 he formed the Cleveland Band, using his brothers, Jimmy and Richard and in later years, his two sons Armin and Martin and opened the Hotel Eden (now the Willerby Manor).

At the moment of writing *The Frank Cleveland Orchestra*, plays regularly to a packed audience at the Springhead pub in Willerby.

Personnel include: Piano: *Eric Seaward Bass: Martin Shaw*. Drums: *Pete Parker, Eric Wright, Dave Harvey, Dean Addinall*.
Trumpets: *Alf Stephenson, Martin Cleveland, Ricky Cleveland, Nigel Davies*.
Trombones: *Dave Howarth, Roy Cooper, Tony Wells, Jeff Holme*.
Sax's: *Frank Cleveland, Peter Bellamy, Mick Richardson, Jim Cleveland, Armin Cleveland*. Vocalist: *Craig Leach*.
Frequent stand-ins include: *George Wilcox* (sax) *Keith Parker* (trumpet) *Pete Reed* and *Becky Bull* (trombone) also *Ray DesForges* (vocals)

THE CRACKAJACKS

The original line-up consisted of *Pete Middleton, Roy Longbottom, Joanne Richardson* (Peters) and *Jean Longbottom*. This was a singing group put together, specifically for a new television talent competition, called 'Top Town'. Hull were asked to appear on the first broadcast. The team was selected by the B.B.C producer Barney Colehan included *Norman Collier, The Richard Twins, Carrie Morley, Maureen Leathley* and *John Brighton*.
The vocalists were backed by a 25-piece orchestra and the listeners voted for the winner.
The programme was listed in the Radio Times, 28th August 1950.
'9,00pm. The best of new radio talent of towns from all parts of the British Isles competing for the title of 'Top Town.'
They finished champions, beating Bristol, but were beaten by Cleethorpes the following Year.
After the show, both *Sheila Edkins* and *Joan Richardson* were asked to appear as solo artists in *George Elrick's* programme, 'When You're Smiling.'
The Crackajacks often appeared in the interval during the dances at many of the local dance halls.

Ken Frith, pianist, wrote a selection of modern arrangements especially for the show. **Barney Colehan**, the producer, told them they he considered them 'a breath of fresh air."

Joanne and Jean left the group and **Sheila Edkins** and **Wynn Hickey** took their places.

The MICKEY CROSS BAND

Personnel included: Sax's: **Len Baron, Ev. Snowden, Les Consitt.** Drums: **Ray Aldridge** and **Mickey**, who was the vocalist also played trumpet.

MAXWELL DANIELS and HIS SWEET MUSIC

Maxwell played at many major events. He won an award from the Melody Maker and became a full time pro. Playing trumpet he graced the stage at London Palladium, The Paradise Club in Oxford St. London and many, prestigious venues, including a tour of the Moss Empire Theatres.

When he returned to Hull he became resident at the Alexandra Hotel, Bridlington and the Duke Of Cumberland, Ferriby.

In a 1952 a publicity leaflet, Max tells would be punters that: "Our repertoire ranges from Old Time to Modern, covering Scottish and Square Dancing and are proud to mention that we were the first augmented orchestra to play Square Dancing locally at Beverley Road Baths where 900 dancers took part."

After leaving the army he gigged around the city but predominately organised dances at Hessle Town Hall. I interviewed him when he was eighty-three and to the best of his knowledge the following musicians were in the original line-up. **Jack Sheard** (bass) **Bobby Wilkinson** (drums) **Harry Bolder** (trumpet) **Horace Holloway** (trombone) **Len Rangely** (Tenor) and **Joanne Richardson** (vocalist) who recalls. "Maxie would be playing his trumpet and suddenly spot someone trying to get in without playing. He would drop his instrument, even in the middle of playing and head off to the offending punter. They either paid or he ejected them, returning as if nothing had happened and start playing again."

Trevor Hickson recalls a time they were playing at the City hall, as backing band to *Vic. Lewis.* "Max could reach top notes without a problem and Vic Lewis was so impressed with his performance that he offered him a contract there and then."

I asked Maxwell why he had given up music after only a few years, but he said it was difficult running a band and all the gigs he was offered were for 3rd trumpet. "I was much more accomplished trumpeter than those on first, so I conceded defeat and retired, but I still occasionally have a blow with *Alan Harmer.*"

It's a shame because many of the musicians I spoke to said he had a superb tone.

HAROLD DAWSON

Harold started playing professionally at the age of 15 and was fronting his own band at 18. In a dance band contest held at the Royal Hall, Bridlington, orchestras from York, Hull, Doncaster and Bradford competed and editor of the Melody maker was one of the judges. Each band had to play three numbers under actual dance conditions. The floor was packed and the judges sat in a screened off corner on the balcony.

Harold and The Cecilian Dance Band took third place, but three of the band were awarded medals for the best individual performance. These were *Tom Ford*, tenor saxophone; *Stan Thornham*, bass: and Harold himself as pianist.

He then decided to build up a bigger and better type of band from Hull's very proficient musicians.

The results justified his perseverance. His new band gained success after success in contests throughout the North of England, taking runners-up in the All-Yorkshire championship. His line up for that evening was three saxes, two trumpets, piano, bass and drums. This time it was trumpet, trombone and bass which took individual honours.

But the following year the band was disqualified. After a complaint by one of the competing bands. They argued that Harold's band was not a bone-fide band within the rules, insomuch as it had not played a dance engagement with that line-up. It was investigated and the judges ruled the complaint justified, even though Harold told them he was using that specific band on numerous bookings already accepted. A few weeks later he ran a large advert; 'Harold Dawson reigns supreme. You must hear our new band. Thursday 8 to 12 and Saturday 8 to 11.30.'

In competitions around England the band won a total of over 80 cups and medals.

During the war Powolny's Restaurant and ballroom was completely destroyed by a bomb and all the band's equipment, together with Harold's vast library of music and a multitude of special orchestrations.

The band reformed and opened up at the White House Hotel.

After the war the military authorities derequisitioned the New York ballroom and *Harold Dawson* was asked to be the musical director. In the late 40's he ran the resident band for four years at the New York Hotel, under the name, 'The New Yorkers.'

Their signature tune was 'You and the Night and the Music."

They played for seven nights a week, most were private functions, but the regular dances were held every Wednesday and Saturday. Previously he could be heard at The Newington hall, Albert Avenue.

In 1946, at a charity show at Hull New Theatre, in aid of the Hull City Police Boys Clubs', five bands were on stage but Harold topped the bill.

Wilf. Camplejohn used to play everybody's pad. *Trevor Hickson* said: "We could have just sat there and mimed letting Wilf. play the lot. If you were a bit dubious about a new number, he'd jump in and say, I'll play that.'

The drummer *Pete Wainwright* was only fifteen years old when he took over from *Stan Blackshaw*. I was also told that *George Footitt* was known as "Tearaway," but no-one knew why.

Didn't live up to his nick-name then.

Wynn Hickey said: Harold was like *Tommy Fisher* and would read a paper while playing. He scanned every word written in the Sports Mail. He would leave it on the top of the piano, as if it was music and happily tinkle away, while avidly reading the contents, turning over pages while playing." She giggled. "But that was nothing. He used to play with his arms at full stretch, leaning dangerously back on his chair, until it was balanced precariously on two legs, on at least three occasions, Harold mis-took his balance and shot off the stage. All the band ignored him and he just looked rather bemused, climbed back and carried on as if nothing had happened."

Harold's band was playing at the Fulford when a punter kept asking if he could sing with the band. Harold declined his offer, but he became so insistent, he relented.

"He told us what the song was, but as you can guess he hadn't a clue what key he wanted. We started up and it was pretty obvious the one thing that man couldn't do was sing! But as they do, he kept on. Punters yelling 'Get him off,' didn't help matters. He ended up very embarrassed and crept off back stage, ending up in the small dressing room, where he climbed out of the window to escape facing the rest of the dancers but he was apprehended by two passing policeman."

"I've been singing with the band," he told them.

"Oh, yes," said the doubtful constables.

He was marched through the hall for everyone to see. When they reached the stage, in a very loud voice, a policeman asked, "Has this fellah been singing with you?"

His embarrassment was compounded even more when almost as one voice the band shouted.

" No, he hasn't."

Eric Wright said: "*Harry Robb* was the trombonist for Harold and he often would turn up with dirt and chalk all over his clothes. We found out his wife would throw his instrument between two asbestos garages and there was only about a foot between them, but he would only find out minutes before he was leaving the house so had to retrieve it in his band gear."

Frank Cleveland laughed. "That's nothing, one day he turned up at the New York Hotel minus his instrument. 'Sorry,' he told Harold, 'I can't play tonight, my wife's buried my trombone in the garden and she wont tell me where it is."

Harry Robb used to go to all the gigs on a motorbike, with his trusty trombone lashed to the back. They'd been invited to play at Goole baths and so the band all crammed into a car, with Harry following behind. Upon arrival at the baths, they found they'd forgotten the dots. Harold was despatched on his motor bike to retrieve the pad. The band left it as long as they could before taking the stage, but the punters were getting restless.

"The problem was," said *Wynn Hickey*, " we could only ad-lib one number. First it was played as a vocal, we had a short break, then tried it with the band only. We had another short break and I got up to sing again. We were panicking a bit by now as there was still no sign of Harry with the lost dots. Our bandleader had a brainwave, he muttered to me, 'How about trying it as a quickstep Wynn? But thankfully before I had time to think about it the welcome sight of Harold, with music tucked under his arm, could be seen rushing through the assembled throng. The trouble was," said Wynn, "nobody had noticed anything untoward."

"Do you remember the time halter necks were all the fashion?" asked Wynn. I admitted I did, "Well one evening we were playing for the 'Palais Glide'. *George Footit* who played trumpet, used to make some very strange noises on it when he saw a pretty girl. He lost control completely one night, when in full sight of all the band, a young lady's boobs popped out. She seemed completely unaware of the brough haw she was making, but the band reserved a big cheer for her partner who leant over and tucked them back in."

Line-up included: *Bill Pickles, Fred Wildbore, Wilf Camplejohn, Alf. Thorpe, Reg. Bates, Stan Grey, Johnny Franklin, Frank Cleveland, Geoff Robson.*

Trumpets: *George Footitt, George Mather, Frank Cocking, Billy Clutterbrook*

Trombones: *Harry Robb, Alan Smith, Percy Stather, Horace Holloway*

Rhythm - *Bill Edkins* (Piano), *Frank Ayers* & *Cyril Sellars* (Drums), *Stan Blackshaw, Pete Wainwright* & *Frank Wignall* (Bass), *Arthur Bryant* (Spanish Guitar) *Wynn Hickey* (Vocalist).

TOMMY FISHER

Here was a musician renowned throughout the area. I didn't speak to a musician who didn't have a story about Tommy. I heard it all, from his distinctive tartan jacket, reading a newspaper while playing, taking the boys to a gig on a fire engine or playing the accordion with a broken arm.

The broken arm episode was recalled by *Frank Cleveland*. "We were playing at the Memorial Hall in Beverley and as we were arriving, *Harry Chatterton*, who'd been collecting gear from a gig the previous night, came tottering towards us, walking as usual with two sticks. As we approached him Tom said: "Come on Harry I'll carry your trombone for you.' Don't forget this was while Tom had his arm in a sling, in fact he played the whole night with his arm strapped up." He smiled. "When it was cold, it wasn't unusual to see him tinkling away (I think he meant on the piano!) wearing mittens."

Another musician told me: "When he was playing at Beverley Road Baths he would come straight from his shop at the top of Beverley Road. You would see him sat at the piano eating his sandwiches and reading the paper, which was perched on the music stand. Between munches he'd announce, 'Next dance please' and carry on. Trouble was he couldn't concentrate. He's start off beautifully playing Charmaine, go into another tune, then back to Charmaine and he'd keep popping middle eight's in. But he was a charming bloke and played what the punters wanted."

"Well you know he also used to wear elastic bands around his neck don't you?" asked *Eric Wright*. "The sort kids used to wear on their mittens, the elastic went round his wrist and it helped support his arms."

"He certainly was a character," recalled *Frank Cleveland*. Eric agreed and went on to tell the story about the night at Beverley Road Baths. "I was walking along the long corridor with Chat. and Tom was coming out after collecting his gear from the previous night, wearing a long black coat and homburg hat. "Now Tom how are ya?" asked Harry. "You look like you're carrying for the Coop.' Tom took his hat off and moved to within a foot of Chat. 'Actually Harry I've just buried my father today.' Then putting his hat firmly back on his head, he nodded curtly and walked out.

"I'm so sorry," blurted Chat. "The fact was," said Eric, "that the story wasn't true, but it's the first time I've ever saw Harry Chat. stuck for words."

"Another thing about Tom," recalled *Ricky Cleveland*. "His eyesight was terrible, but it never stopped him driving. One night he told me he'd pick me up at the shop as we had a gig at Hedon. We were beetling along and he was heading straight for the back of a bus. I shouted and he stopped - just! That old shooting brake could carry us all. The vehicle was sort of shared. Whoever lived furthest away got to drop us all off, then the next day they would have to leave it on a bombsight in the centre of Hull. It could be there for four days before Tom picked it up. It had his name plastered all over it. Best advert he had."

"You had it easy," said **R***oy* **Wilkin**, "In the early days, we travelled to most gigs in an old Fordson snub nosed van and in the winter the band would all be in the back huddled around a wick burning paraffin heater. I remember one night we'd all travelled to Withernsea and as we were unloading Tom couldn't find the dots. It was the big band so it was pretty important. He decided he must have left them at home. We were in plenty of time so he turned round and returned to collect them.

He searched his house to no avail and thought he'd have another look in the van. Good job. They'd slipped under the seat, so the journey hadn't been necessary after all."

This memory prompted *Alf Stephenson* to recall another journey to Withernsea which resulted in a flat tyre. "We didn't have a spare, so we filled the thing with grass cuttings. It must be something about that road because another time we were halfway there when I said to Tommy, 'Look at that wheel, shooting along the road. With that the whole car shuddered to a halt. It was ours!"

Tommy would also go to some gigs on his bike. *Frank Cleveland* recalled the time he'd been travelling along Beverley Road and the level crossing gates were about to shut. "He was in a hurry so tried to beat them but the gates scraped all along his legs. They were in a hell of a mess, really badly bruised. Every time he left the stand, Peggy, his wife, who also was his vocalist, knelt on the floor rubbing the circulation back."

Probably the one thing that united all the musicians, was the memory of the many bands Mr Fisher put out. The **Tommy Fisher Orchestra** could be billed at four or five venues on the same night. If he had a band out at the City Hall and Beverley Road Baths, he would step off the stage and walk the length of the ballroom playing his accordion and out of the door at the end, climb on his bike and head for the city centre. Once outside the City Hall he would stride up the long staircase, listen to see what number the band were playing then march the length of the ballroom and up onto the stage, to huge applause. After half-an-hour he would repeat the exercise and return to the original venue. The audience hadn't a clue - probably thought he had a weak bladder - but they loved it and went on blithely thinking they were listening to the original Tommy Fisher Orchestra.

"Sorting out the musicians for line-ups caused more than a few mix-ups, as well," said Frank C. "I know of one gig at the City hall where four bass players turned up."

My favourite story was recalled by the **Cleveland brothers**.
"Tom was out on a gig when he was told to ring his wife at home urgently. Peggy said she'd had a telephone call from a guy wanting to know if Tom could help him out as the band he'd booked hadn't turned up. It was New Year's Eve, so he knew finding a musician, let alone a band was pretty hopeless. 'Let me think now,' said Tom. 'I know, give a few drummers a ring and when you find one free, tell him to take a record player with him and play along with that. Peggy found a drummer who turned up at the gig with drum kit and record player. The best thing was, the organiser of the night wrote him a letter thanking him for a superb evening."

The turn around of band members also caused problems with jackets. The material was so heavy and thick, the musicians likened them to horse blankets. **Ricky Cleveland** said, "It was horrendous if you got one that didn't fit, which was a pretty regular occurrence."

"Also," said **Eric Wright**, "the fact he had so many bands out on the same night, meant he never knew how much he owed you. Musicians would just go up to him and say 'I've come for my wages.' 'How much?' The musician would quote sixty/seventy/eighty pounds and Tom would never query it. He would just reach into his back pocket, peel off the required amount from a large wad and everybody seemed happy. I don't think anybody even thought about fiddling him, he was such a nice guy."

"I don't know about turnaround of jackets," said *Paul Shepherdson*, "I once played with Tom and at the interval we had to take all our gear off stage and lug it all back for the second half."

It's the talk of the town

Alan Bond

And his MUSIC

featuring the MELOMAIDS

Enquiries—'phone:
14562 or 7653
P.T.O.

Frank Cleveland (centre) with his family.
L/R: Brother: Jimmy, Sons: Armin and Martin and brother Ricky

Mike Brown

Crackajacks Mark I
L/R Joan Richardson (Joanne Peters),Pete Middleton, Jean Best, Roy Longbottom, Sheila Edkins

Crackajacks Mark II
L/R: Wynn Hickey, Pete Middleton, Jean Best, Roy Longbottom, Sheila Edkins

Maxwell Daniels and his Sweet Music

Drums: Bert Hickey - Bass: George Thomson - Piano: Len Hanson

Harry Chatterton at the National Dance Band Championships.
Piano: Bill Kinsey - Bass: Bert Boots - Vocalist: Sheila Kinsey

The Mike Brown Orchestra

THE FLEDGLINGS

This was a band formed in 1945. Most of the experienced musicians had been called up, so this which gave a great opportunity to up and coming youngsters. Every Saturday night saw them blowing at the Park St Headquarters for the A.T.C. They received the princely sum of 7/6 (37p) a night.

They were often asked to perform at the Army and Air Force Stations in the area, ably assisted by Millie Littlewoods dancers, much to the delight of the band members. Johnson's Coaches of Hedon laid on transport for them.

Colin Shakespeare said they were returning home one night after an army base gig, in which they had been expected to entertain the troops in a giant marquee, which had been placed over what he described as 'a quagmire'. Millie's dancers had to change in nearby tents and scuttle backwards and forwards to the makeshift stage, in the driving rain.

"On our way home, we'd just reached the outskirts of Hull when the air-raid sirens started. The driver parked quickly beside an air-raid shelter and took cover inside, the girls followed, but we decided to get some 'kip' in the bus. A hour and a half later, the all clear sounded and we were on our way again."

He went on, "Another time because it was winter and bitterly cold, about half-an hour before we arrived they'd lit a fire, fuelled by a large amount of coke. We'd only been playing about five minutes when we came to a coughing spluttering halt. Black smoke billowed everywhere. It took over half-an hour to clear it, which they managed by opening all the doors and windows. Playing in a refrigerator would have had more appeal."

Personnel included: Piano. *Norman Mail*. Bass:*Arthur Grant*. Drums: *Ray Johnson*

Trumpets: *Dave Mitch, Dennis Johnson*

Saxes: *Bernard Collinson* (Tenor) *Colin Shakespeare* (2nd tenor)

Dennis & *Ray Johnson* & *Bob* and *Arthur Grant* were brothers, but soon this band also became depleted by conscription. *Norman Mail* and *Colin Shakespeare* the first to go.

75

JOHNNY FRANKS BAND

This was a big band formed in 1947, playing for Saturday night dances at East Hull baths. Musicians in his original line-up were:

Drums/band leader: *Johnny Franks*. Bass: *Bert Boots*. Piano: *Les Rowson*.
Trumpets: *Maxwell Daniels. Johnny Cowper.*
Saxes: *Tony Bolton, Doug Sewell, Les Horncastle, George Appleyard.*
Vocalists: *Joanne Richardson* and *Don Holden.*

Jo Richardson said she had a wonderful time with all the bands she sang with, "But it must be me, because weird and wonderful things seem to happen when I'm around."

"For instance?" I asked.

" I did a great deal of theatre work, and I was appearing at the Tivoli Theatre in Hull. Top of the bill was *Old Mother Riley* and *Kitty McShane.* They'd been arguing pretty forcibly all day," said Joanne. "I was in the wings waiting for my entrance after one of his spots. He had just got to the side where I was waiting, when he dropped dead at my feet."

AMBROSE GIBBINS AND HIS ORCHESTRA

This was one of the top bands in the 30's and 40's, playing every Saturday night at Hessle Town Hall.

One of the regulars, Jean, used to have at least four dances with the M.C. "I was forever singing as we danced around the floor. One night he told me Arthur (professionally known as Ambrose) was looking for a vocalist. We were introduced and not only did I go on to sing with him but I also became his wife, the rest as they say is history." She recalled "After the last waltz at the end of the evening we always played the National anthem and no-one moved a muscle. We all then used to get on our bikes and cycle home. I remember the Hessle copper was called *Dick Huddleston* and he used to always tell my parents when he'd seen me. 'I don't know where your daughter had been but she was singing at the top of her voice going down Beverley Road."

"Did Arthur cycle to the dances?"

"Every one. After the war he was resident at the White House Hotel for six years. They called it 'The White House Swingtette.'

Line-up: Piano: **Arthur Gibbins**. Orchestrations/bass: **Jimmy Stewart**
Drums/vibraphone: **Jack Lee**
Sax and clarinet: **Fred Rawson**. Guitar: **Jack Leng**.

"Arthur and I lived at Ganstead, outside Hull," said Jean, "but he still cycled to gigs. After work, he'd rush home, have his tea, never had time for a pudding, then get washed. His tuxedo was laid out on the bed and his shoes cleaned. He put them on and shoot off."

"What in his tuxedo?"

"Oh yes, with a huge trench coat on top. He was playing six nights a week and was paid £9.00. In fact his very first gig was at Aldbrough. It was in an amusement arcade and they moved all the slot machines to one side to make room for the dancers. Arthur and his drummer Jackie Lee cycled several times all the way from Hull to play.

As well as his orchestra Arthur, started a trio to play for dancing at the Fulford Rooms, Beverley Road, it consisted of Arthur playing piano, **Jackie Lee** on drums and **Kenny Baker** on trumpet.

Jean said Arthur never smoked or drank but regular punters didn't know this and would line up drinks for him on the piano. **Jack Leng** the guitarist was delighted. He scoffed the lot.

LOUIS GOLD AND HIS MONARCH'S OF MELODY

They had a regular Saturday night-spot at the City Hall. Louis was a great showman, always immaculate in evening dress and ready to do a turn. His brother Jerry, became a great comedian, his first professional engagement was in a Sheffield pub, he gave two shows a day for a week, and was paid three pounds. The Gold's cloth, linings and button business in Osborne St, supplied most of the tailors in Hull. This was a thriving area, with Scandinavian food stores, wine and fruit shops, barbershops and of course fish and chips. Hammond's, **Maurice Coupland** and Goldstones all started out in Osborne Street. Italians sold ice cream in the summer and roast chestnuts in the winter. Popular with all the children were the organ grinders with their monkeys.

Jerry recalled playing soccer at Osborne Street school. "They always put me in goal. I was so fat and chubby, I took up most of the goalmouth. It was the toilet doorway, a yard wide!"

On a Thursday afternoon, half-day closing, it was free entertainment in the Cosmopolitan Club in George Street. *Joe Hyman*, who was the local barber, would be challenged to a dancing and singing contest, by another local barber, *Moisha Krantz*. Bets and side bets would be laid, *Louis Golding* was the pianist and the winner was announced by the amount of applause each received.

Pandemonium would break out if Moisha was declared the winner, so they had to hold the contest over again. To keep the peace it was always declared a dead heat.

CERES & EDWIN HARPER

Edwin was a familiar figure in Bridlington. This was in the days when band leaders were always impeccably turned out in tails. His sister said Ceres always had his suits made at *Leonard Silver* in Hull. "He used to have numerous fittings before it was ready. He'd gone for a final fitting and they found the left sleeve was slightly longer than the right, so they duly marked it and told him it would be ready for collection at the end of the week. Ceres called in and collected the suit all 'bagged up' and ready for him. He put it in the wardrobe and it was nearly two weeks later before he was ready to wear his spanking new suit. After a bath and shave he put on his new suit, but oh calamity, they'd only taken up the normal sleeve and it looked ridiculous. As it was Saturday he had to wait 'till Monday before he could complain, so it was back to his shiny old one."

She suddenly said: "Oh by the way did you know he's buried in Sewerby churchyard and on his headstone he has notes of music and the words 'Thanks For The Memory,' which was also the signature tune of Bob Hope."

HARRY HOPPER and His Famous Olde Tyme Orchestra

St. John's Church Hall in Rosemead St., was a regular venue followed by the City Hotel, Lowgate, then went on to play gigs throughout the region. When the Locarno Ballroom opened he played for a V.IP ball.

No-one could recall any personnel for this band.

ALAN HURST ORCHESTRA

Opened in the 50's, this was the original resident band for the Majestic Ballroom, Witham. All were out of town professionals, but gradually local semi-pro's were introduced.

IBSON LEN

Played at the Assembly Rooms, Newington Hall, Jackson's Ballroom and the Metropole Dance Hall.

Len played Saxophone with *Fred Rounding, Jack Cooper* and *Mick Cross* on vocals and trumpet.

JAZZ VEHICLE

This is a big band, which comprises of nearly all the musicians who played during the golden days of dance halls. All enjoy a blow with *Alf Stephenson's* big band most Saturday mornings at the Springhead Pub in Anlaby. I went along to a rehearsal and all the lads were in top form, with anecdotes coming thick and fast.

During the rehearsal a piece had to be played over and over again. The trumpets were having a hard time, when the keyboard player, *Eric Seaward* was heard to heave a quiet sigh, *Keith Parker* took it personally. "All you do is press a key and a bloody note comes out," he told him. The trumpets had another stab at the difficult passage. "Don't forget the creme-de-la-creme is playing now," said *Norman Baron.*

"What as well as the trumpet players?" asked *Ray DesForges*.

Ray is well known for his ready quips. Alf recalled the time a manager came to tell the band he'd had complaints about the acoustics. Quick as a flash, Ray shouted. "Have you put traps down?"

Later, an insect was buzzing around the room, suddenly landing on *John Mallinder's* music. "Was it a bee?" asked Alf. "No, B-flat," shouted Ray Des.

Alf also recalled the time they had a get together to discuss arrangements at his house.

"*John Mallinder* asked if he could make a coffee. After a few minutes he called out, 'Why is there an empty milk bottle in the fridge?"

"In case anyone wants black coffee," somebody shouted.

"I don't want him making my coffee," said *Ray DesForges*.

"Why?"

"He suffers from Hermes."

"Don't you mean Herpes?"

"No, Hermes, he's a carrier. Well he always carries my gear."

All members of the band were going to a gig at Wigan and Alf had hired a mini-bus.

They were all settled in the bus for the return journey and Ray DesForges sat at the front with Alf, who was driving, telling him. "Don't worry Alf. I'll keep you awake."

Alf laughed and said: "Guess who was the first to fall asleep. Bloody DesForges."

THE KINGSTON SAXAPHONE QUARTET

Formed by *Richard Lamb* (Soprano) it included *Colin Shakespeare* (Alto) *Les Horncastle* (tenor) and *Wilf Camplejohn* (Baritone), this was successful for several years, but Richard had to leave Hull and as they were unable to find another soprano player the ensemble was disbanded. In 1997 a new quartet was formed. The line up *Mike Button* (Soprano) *Noel Weston* (Tenor) *John Mallinder* (Baritone) and the only original member, *Colin Shakespeare* (Alto)

BILL KINSEY BAND

Bill played nothing but orchestral music until he was seventeen, then suddenly switched to dance tempo. During his five years in the army, he spent four years as a Prisoner of War in Germany, where he formed and led an Orchestra of 23 instrumentalists in the Prison Camp.

They were resident for several years at the Regal Ballroom, Beverley, then to the New York Hotel for two years, taking over from *Harold Dawson*, followed by two years at the Royal Station Hotel, Ferensway

Bill was a stickler for correct dress. *Eric Wright* said: "One night *Trevor Hickson* turned up wearing brown shoes. "'You can't go on stage wearing those,' Bill told. 'That's ridiculous' said Trevor. 'I'm at the back, nobody will see them.' Eventually Bill let him stay but warned him if it happened again he'd get the sack! Actually," said Eric, "a similar thing happened to me. Each section wore a different coloured jacket for the Tuesday and Saturday gigs at the Beverley Regal. I'd turned up in grey and it should have been red. It was about half-an-hour before the start but Bill insisted I go home and change. I refused and when he got insistent, I shoved my sticks in his hand and told him I would play in grey or not at all. I played."

I asked Sheila how she became a vocalist for the band. "Bill had a gig at the Duke Of Cumberland and asked if I'd like to go with him for an evening out. I got dressed up to the nines, with a long dress, as we had been told it was a formal evening. When I entered the room, not one other female was in a full-length dress. I was mortified and felt so conspicuous. Bill understood my embarrassment and asked if I'd like to sing a few numbers. I'd often had a go at home, but this was different. But," as Sheila said, "anything was better than looking so out of place and the singer was expected to wear long frocks, so I was delighted to give it a go, and the rest is history."

Walkington Village Hall brought back memories for many of the boys.
"It would be 1960 or '61 and in the centre of the stage was a large pot bellied stove, we all had to plant ourselves around it and sweated profusely the whole night."

"The bit I remember that night," interrupted *Ray DesForges*, "was at the beginning when a man went up to Bill and asked if he could play with the band. Bill ummd and aahhed a bit but eventually agreed. He played every number with us, even a slow waltz on the SPOONS!"

Another time they were playing in an upstairs room at a hall in Howden. The boys noticed a door at the side of the stage so went to investigate. It was a fire escape. At the interval they persuaded the alto player *Ev. Snowden* to have a look outside. He stepped out only to hear the door slam behind him. It was pitch dark and all Ev. could see were the lights below, with no indication of any stairs. By the time they let him back in he was a gibbering wreck.

In July 1957, *Trevor Hickson* was one of the first confirmed polio cases in Hull. For three weeks it was touch and go. He said, "I knew in the first week that if I stopped trying I would be put into the iron lung, but, although my chest was inactive, I managed with what little use I had left in the diaphragm to draw in enough air to keep myself alive."

Trevor was told that, in order to endeavour to control the disease, his temperature must be kept down and he was to lie motionless for two to three weeks.

After a few days, the nurses at Castle Hill Hospital, Cottingham, were attracted to a strange rattling noise. It was Trevor kicking at the bed rail, already attempting to get some reaction from his motionless legs.

He had a bet with the nurses - that he would walk alone within a month of being struck down. It was a bet they hope they'd lose. And lose it they did. As Trevor said, "If you want a thing badly enough, then you've got to damn well go out and get it. It's no good sitting around. It was probably something to do with brute strength and ignorance." Although within three weeks his weight had fallen from a robust 13st 10lb to 7st 8lb.

He was moved to the Westwood Hospital in Beverley where he began a course of physiotherapy. It was excersise, excersise, excersise. One day some musician friends went to visit him. "Get my trumpet from the bedside cupboard," he told a pal, "Right chaps, sit back and I'll give you a tune."

He took a deep breath, placed the instrument to his lips and blew.

Not even the breath could be heard coming out of the bell of the trumpet as he strained to produce a note. "Ah, well," he said, "I'll have another bash in a couple of days."

He never did give up the idea of playing, he kept his mouthpiece in his dressing gown pocket, so he could get in a bit of practise whenever the occasion arose.

After three months he was allowed home. His wife Olive had made arrangements for him to sleep downstairs, but Trevor had other ideas, "I know I was being bloody stubborn, but I was convinced I could get up those stairs somehow."

Twenty minutes later, he was beginning to have his doubts, he was till three stairs off the top. His wife couldn't help as he felt extreme pain every time he was touched. He made one last effort and reached the top. "My grin must have been a mile wide," he said, "but I knew I could do it."

The same agonising climb continued night after night. He admitted, "It was two months before I could manage them reasonably easily."

In February 1958 he returned to work at the Hull typewriter factory, albeit in a much lighter job, than his original tool-setter.

He obtained a specially made trumpet, which he had adapted for left-handed playing. It was much more lightly balanced than his previous instrument.

The band used to play at Imperial Typewriters."But," said Trevor, "the roof was built in great undulating curves and when you blew, it bounced off the ceiling and the sound came back to you a beat and a half later."

Trevor won Opportunity Knocks and it led to an acting role in a James Bond spoof, 'Thunderbag.' He told me: "I played Bugsy Flange and I was shot by a Greek in Lowestoft."
Not a lot I can say to that Trevor.

As many of the dance hall musicians, Trevor gives regular lessons to the local up and coming youngsters. He told me "I've taught for thirty years and in that time only five failed their exams."

Ray Scott (alto) got married on a Saturday and he had gone to London for a few days honeymoon, but had to return on the Thursday as the Kinsey band had a gig at Withernsea Pavilion.

"Not too much of a problem, you might think," said Ray, "except *Ray DesForges* had, as usual, been chatting up a girl and she had invited him back for coffee! She obviously lived in Withernsea and again you'd think no problem. Wrong! Ray had given me a lift and didn't tell me about the new arrangements until the rest of the band had gone. It was bloody awful," recalls Ray Scott. "Here I was on my honeymoon and I was drinking coffee with some strange woman, while my new wife, Mavis, was at home waiting eagerly for my return. It was years before I dare tell her."

Sheila Edkins, Bill's wife, recalls the time they were playing for the Woolshippers on the City of York, moored on King George Dock. "It was free drink and food, which could not be passed up by many of the musicians." The drummer *Eric Wright* admitted he was paralytic. "Can you imagine free booze to musicians. I was drinking brandy and champagne! But Bill said I still played a passable set even though I was playing parry diddles on *Ray DesForges's* head. Half way through the evening, *Trevor Hickson* went missing. Bill was very concerned so sent a steward to see if he could find him. Not a sign. We all knew he'd had too much to drink and Bill was convinced he'd fallen into the dock, so he apologised to the dancers, explained the situation and said they couldn't carry on playing as they had to find him. For over two hours, dancers and band scoured the docks looking for our lost musician. They found his car but no Trevor. We eventually went home convinced he'd met a watery end. Bill was furious the following day to find out that he'd been found wandering around earlier by the Dock police. They couldn't get any sense out of him, except where he lived, so they made sure he was returned home safely. He was no doubt sleeping soundly, while we were all freezing to death in a howling east wind looking for him."

In fact," continued Sheila," Bill was so angry he sacked him, but we missed him. He returned for a short while then went to pastures new. He was a lovely fellah, but he did like the booze," recalls Sheila.

I checked the story with Trevor and giving me a cheeky grin he said: "Can't deny it. But I'm in good company. Did you know *Harry James* knocked back a bottle of vodka a night and he could still knock 'em dead."

Bert Boots recalled: "While we were playing at the Beverley regal, we were approached by members of the US Air base and asked if we'd like a gig at Driffield, when we'd finished. They offered a spanking wage plus all the ale we could drink, so we'd do eight 'till one, then head off for the Sergeants Club. The first time we went to Driffield, we played from two to six am, well all except *Ray DesForges* the tenor player. He was driving round the base completely lost. Suddenly he came across some rockets and was terrified he was in a high security area. He was convinced he would be arrested. Eventually he found the hall and for the first time in his life, the teetotal Mr DesForges, downed a very welcome Cherry Vodka, followed by another and another. Well that's his story anyway.

We started the gig with Basie's, 'Lil Darlin' and from that moment we couldn't do a thing wrong. The Yanks loved us."

I asked what the musicians were paid for a gig. "In the fifties and sixties we were all out just about every single night and for a Saturday night we usually got thirty shillings (£1.50) but if we were playing 'till one or two in the morning we got £2.00."

Sheila, a natural blonde, remembers the time she thought, just for a change, she would try out a dark brown wig. She wore it for four nights, when Bill asked her to go back to being blonde.

"Why? I asked, as I liked it."

"Bill told me, 'A punter came up to me last night and asked where the blonde singer was, then he told me she was a bloody sight better than the dark haired bird."

Although nothing to do with Bill's band, it ties in with a story told to me by *Paul Shepherdson*. "We were making our way from the dressing room along a dimly lit corridor and the girl singer was wearing a wig, it was whipped off by a nail stuck out of the wall. The musician behind retrieved it and plonked it back on. 'You look great' we told her." He was smiling rather mischievously so I didn't have to ask any more!

The musicians who played regularly for Bill included:
Band leader/piano: *Bill Kinsey* (Edkins)
Drums: *Eric Wright*. Bass: *Bert Boots*. Piano: *Bill Edkins*.
Trumpets: *Trevor Hickson, Brian Hargrave, Dave Mitchell.*
Sax's: *Len Rangely, Dennis Proby, Ray Scott, Johnny Grindley, Ray DesForges.*

IVOR KIRCHIN BAND

This was a professional band brought in to open up the Locarno Ballroom on Ferensway, Hull. It was made up mainly of out of town musicians. All the boys came to the city with pre-conceived ideas. "It smells of fish." "It's a city that goes nowhere" or as one trumpeter remarked. "That God-forsaken place." But as many before them, they soon became integrated into our city with its woodlands, hills, beaches and foreign parts just a whisper away.

Norman Baron told me, "One night as the curtain went up, the rotating stage ground to a halt. The brass section of one band was playing them out and the rhythm section of the returning band playing themselves in, problem was they were both playing different tunes."

Norman continued. "A few of us worked on Hull Fish Dock to earn extra money," he then gave me a cheeky grin and told me it was, "to pay for our divorces." He went on, "Some of the pro's would meet in the afternoon and go along to see a film. One day we decided to go to a cinema where they were showing the film of a recent heavyweight title fight. We all settled in our seats, when I felt a hand on my thigh, it slowly moved upwards, forever upwards. I couldn't believe it," said Norman, "I could just make out the features of a rather attractive female, so I didn't complain! I'm sure it was an absorbing heavyweight contest, but I must admit I didn't take a lot of notice."

"But back to stories about the band," said Norman. " One night I hadn't had time to relieve myself during the interval - well I had but I'd used it for drinking time! - We weren't supposed to but I smuggled a pint glass onto the stand and sure enough within ten minutes I was bursting. *Donny Keith* was giving a Sinatra song the works, when I seized my opportunity. I turned away from the dancers and started peeing into the glass, except the bloody thing was filling like Niagara Falls, so I grabbed my mute and filled that as well. I had just completed and was zipping back up when we were called into action. Luckily trumpeters are at the back because you could quite clearly see a flash of my green underpants. I had my come-uppance though. I had to use my mute and the bloody thing spilled all over my band suit. Cost me pounds to have the thing cleaned."

Noel Flint (bass) told me he'd asked **Albert Harrison** if he would dep. for him, because he was too ill to appear. "Albert was terrified at the thought as he'd had no experience playing with a big band. He was stood on the revolving stage waiting to take over from the trio, which had been performing at the start of the evening, but he was standing too near the edge of the stage and as it started to revolve his music caught the wall and tipped all over. *Eddie Grey* gathered it up in one hand while still playing the piano with the other and handed it back to Albert. It only took a few seconds to sort it out and he was ready to go when then they'd reached the centre. Albert likened it to playing football for England when you'd only had experience with a Sunday league team. Blisters appeared within half-an-hour and his fingers were numb."

Noel also told me: "Albert said he never slept a wink that night as he just kept playing the tunes over and over in his head. In fact it was Noel who gave Albert and *Fred Harrison* lessons. He recalls: "They used to come to my house on cycles, with their instruments perched in a trailer they'd knocked up. I think Al bought his from *Harry Chatterton* for fifteen pounds and Fred had popped in to see what *Pat Cornell* had to offer. He got two for ten pounds as they were in a right state. One with no strings. But he managed to patch them up. Not a bad buy."

Donnie Keith the vocalist had sang for as long as he could remember. Touring with many famous bands of the era. He had some entertaining tales to tell.

"I was performing in a club with a local dance band. In the middle of 'Fly Me To The Moon,' we were raided by the police. The entire band was shepherded into a nearby room and our names and addresses taken. The young copper, with pencil poised was ready for action.

A sax. player moved forward.
Copper: Name please.
Musician: **Tommy Plunkett**
The next sax. player moved forward.
Copper: Name please.
Musician: **Terry Slogitt**.
A trumpet player was next in line.
Copper: Name please.
Musician: **Tommy Smith**

Another trumpet player moved forward.

Copper: Name please.

Musician: *Tommy Smith*

At this the policeman blew his top. 'I've had enough of this s***t. Now can we start again and this time I want no bloody messing about and proper names."

"Trouble was," said Donny, "They were their proper names. I couldn't help laughing because the previous night we'd had a *Teddy Pratt* playing for us and the clarinettist was called *Cyril Tudge*."

I had to admit that was some line up. Although Plunkett and Slogitt were perfect for a firm of solicitors. I know Tommy Smith was a footballer, but I'm saying nothing about Tudge and Pratt.

Line-up included:

Fronting the band: *Ivor Kirchin*.

Piano/arranger: *Eddie Gray*. Bass:*Brian Wiltshire, Noel Flint*. Drums: *Fred Ashworth*.

Trumpets: *Norman Baron, Alan Downey, Ray Lynam,, Donny Morgan*.

Sax's: *Denis Terenzio, Tony Tears, Brian Suttill, Gill Monk. George Wilcox*

Vocalist: *Donny Keith*.

The GEOFF LAYCOCK BAND

This outfit played mostly in Scarborough but the musicians were all from Hull. They were playing at the Floral Hall, when the organiser asked Geoff if the band could play until two am. At 2.03am, Geoff asked *Ray DesForges* to sing one more number as the disc jockey hadn't arrived. As he started, "We'll Meet Again," *John Mallinder* picked up his sax and music stand and marched off the stage muttering. "Oh no we ******* wont."

Well he did live at Ottringham, and as the owner of a paper shop had to be up at 5am. But there was a problem, he'd gone with *Ray DesForges*, so he had to stand in a freezing carpark - don't forget this was November, not to be recommended with the wind howling in from the North Sea - for another half-an-hour. Needless to say he was not amused.

Geoff was renowned for getting dates and venues mixed up. *Donny Keith* recalls the time he'd rang members of the band to tell them they had a gig in Cleethorpes. It was the annual Policeman's Ball. He suggested they all meet in a car park and follow him to the venue.

Roy Cooper, the trombone player was in the car with Geoff. They arrived at Cleethorpes but couldn't find the hall. Suddenly Roy spotted a policeman. "Quick, ask him," he said. They pulled up beside the copper and Geoff asked where the dance was being held. "We're the band you've booked," explained Geoff. "I don't think so," said the policeman, "That's tomorrow night." Are you sure?" The copper radioed in and confirmed it was the following night.

"Bloody Hell," said Geoff, "What shall I tell the lads? I've got to have time to think." They were near a roundabout, so he waved his arm out of the window, that signalled, 'follow me.' "We did, three times around the bloody thing," said Donny

Eventually he headed down a side road and stopped outside a pub. "Sorry lads, I've got the wrong night, its tomorrow, but let's not waste the evening, come inside and I'll treat you all to a drink."

Problem. Only one of the musicians could do the next night, they all had confirmed gigs with other bands.

That's similar to what happened to me," said *Ray DesForges*. "Geoff. had rung up to book me for the 23rd of December in York. "Are you sure? I asked him. Nobody books a dance for the 23rd. But he was adamant. 'I've got the confirmation letter,' he told me.

"We all headed for York, only to be met by Geoff waving frantically outside the venue. "Sorry lads, It's the wrong night. It's tomorrow."

Needless to say not one musician was available for Christmas Eve. "We never found out what he told the organisers," said Ray, "because anybody who could hold an instrument was already booked."

This brought another reminiscence from *Donny Keith*. "We were playing at Scarborough and he'd booked a new drummer who lived in Hull, so I offered to give him a lift. I'd heard he was an excellent musician, but had never heard or met him before. We'd done about fifteen minutes of the first set, long enough to find out the drummer was c**p. Geoff called for an interval. Everybody complained bitterly about the new member. 'Sorry lads but what can I do?' Geoff told the barman to 'look after my boys.' Don't forget this was a big band with five saxes, five trumpets, four trombones and the rest. They were all imbibing freely, so I hate to think what the bar bill cost. The drummer kept returning and asking when we were going on, but we all ended up so pissed, we never did manage to play another note - not me, I'm tee-total - I then realised I had brought the drummer to the gig and I'd have to hold a conversation with him all the way back to Hull, so decided to kip down at a mates in Scarborough. I rang my wife and explained, telling the drummer I didn't feel well enough to drive home."

"You didn't leave him to make his own way did you?" I asked.

"No, it's all right, there were quite a few Hull lads there. I can't remember for sure, but it was either *John Mallinder* or *Alf Stephenson* that did the decent thing."

Len Ibson and his Band at the Metropole 1933

Johnny Franks' Band

White House Hotel 1943
L/R: Dep. from RAF Leconfield - Ambrose Gibbins, Jack Leng, Fred Rawson

Steve Marshall's Contemporary Jazz Sounds

Ivor Kirchin Band

94

Bill Kinsey Band, Goole Baths, 1961
Trumpets: Keith Parker, Alf Stephenson, Brian Hargrave
Saxs: Ray Desforges, Dennis Proby, Rob Kurring, Ray Fletcher

Bill Kinsey Orchestra, Goole Baths, 1960
Bass: Bert Boots - Drums: Larry Booth - Vocals: Sheila Edkins

L/R: Fred Adamson, Brian Hargrave, John Mallinder, Paul Gibbins, Ray Desforges, Geoff Laycock

The Cumberland Players
Drums: Bert Hickey - Tenor: Roy Longbottom - Piano: Frank Harrison - Vocals: Wynn Hickey

The Bill Kinsey Orchestra at Beverley Regal Ballroom 1950s

New York Hotel
L/R Bill Kinsey, Alf Stephenson, Bert Boots, Larry Booth

featured with
The BILL KINSEY BAND

Tel: 74701

L/R: Harry Thorney, Brian Hargrave, Alf Stephenson, Dennis Whitehead, Keith Parker

Workshop organised by the Musicans' Union
L/R: Al Jenner, Brian Hargrave, Keith Parker, Norman Baron, Pete Power

Workshop organised by the Musicians' Union
L/R John Mallinder, Mick Richardson, George Wilcox, Lennie Rangely, Ray
Desforges

THE RAY LESTER BAND

A popular band in the 'Forties'.

Ray told me: "It was not unusual to see **Vernon Turner** sitting on the stand, always with a penknife close at hand, chiselling away at his reeds in between sets."

He also recalled the time when he was depping and was having a word with the singer, asking what key he sang in. "No idea," was the reply. Just do what you think," They started up and Ray realised he'd struck lucky and the key was fine for the vocalist. Suddenly a pause by the singer, who leant backwards and whispered, "We're not catching a bloody bus." I'd been so delighted at finding the right key, I'd been playing faster and faster."

His wife **Joanne Richardson** (Peters) giggled and asked if he remembered the time they were playing at Withernsea Pavilion. "You mean the time you borrowed that evening dress?" Jo. nodded. He continued. "Well this dress was miles too long and as we went to set up, Jo carried in the cymbals for us. Diners were already seated and tucking into their meal at the far end of the hall. Suddenly Joanne tripped over the hem of the dress, dropping the cymbals, which went booling along the whole length of the hall, coming to rest at the feet of a diner. It got a huge cheer and Joanne was applauded as she went to collect them from the surprised 'punter'.

"We went everywhere on bikes," said Ray, I would carry the music on my handlebars, Dennis had his accordion on his handlebars and Lester had a small cart made which he could get his drums in. It attached to his bike and away we'd go, but we had a problem with Joanne. She couldn't ride a bike properly. She was all right when she got going but couldn't start or stop, so Vernon was the one elected to catch her at the other end. He would stand in front of her and catch hold of the handlebars, sometimes with painful consequences. The boys always said, when Vernon eventually goes to see his Maker, they'll know it's him because there'll be tyre marks imprinted on his thighs and I've cleaned that up a bit," laughed Ray.

"It doesn't matter," I said, "I think we get the picture."

He also recalled the time he and **Dennis Snee** were cycling along Holderness Road coming home from a gig, when the heavens opened.

"We were getting soaked and I was desperately trying to protect the pad. Suddenly we came to the part on Holderness Road were they parked the buses in the middle of the road. Perfect. We just leant our bikes on the side of a bus, hopped on board and waited for it to finish."

He went on with the reminisces. "We played regularly at Sutton Army Camp and they used to send a truck to pick us up. It would be waiting on Bricknell Ave. But before we got on they made us sign a paper, absolving them of any blame if we were killed. It was nearly always a learner driver and one time he missed a turning, drove across a field and suddenly we had this almighty crash. We were thrown about in the back, but he never stopped. When we got to Sutton, we asked him what had happened. "Ran into a bloody cow." he told us. Did you kill it? 'Why did you fancy some rump steak? he asked."

They had a few attempts at making a record, straight onto the black vinyl. They went to Peel Street, where a fitter from Brough Aerospace had built his own small studio.

"He made violins, so he was pretty useful," said *Ray Richardson*. "Trouble was there was no balance and it had to be done on one take. We were recording and there was supposed to be a guitar solo from Ray Lester, but unbeknown to anyone else a string had broken, so when nothing was forthcoming from Lester, *Ray Richardson* tried a bit of improvisation. The recording was finished and we all looked at Lester, he turned saying, "My bloody string broke." Trouble was," said Ray, "we were still recording, so now everybody knew!"

Line-up: Leader/piano: *Ray Richardson*.
Drums: *Lester Atak*. Bass: *Benny Cheeseman*. Accordian: *Dennis Snee*.
Guitar: *Vic Cheeseman*. Alto:*Vernon Turner* (alto)
Vocals: *Joanne Richardson*.

NORMAN MAIL

When I spoke to Norman he was full of reminiscences: "Apart from being the mainstay at all the Hull University dances, I was resident at the Grange Park Hotel for twenty-four years and the Blind Institute for fourteen years. "In fact it was at the blind," he told me, "that *Keith Parker's* seat suddenly collapsed. He ended up on the floor, but the boys just kept on playing. Keith stood up and carried on blowing. Then the manager came and put another chair in its place. Parker sat down just as the set was finishing. Good job because the lads were now nearly hysterical, but they never missed a note.

We travelled all over in the early days and fog was often a problem. Once we'd just finished a gig at Withernsea Pavilion and came out to a pea-souper. Now that road is pretty hairy at the best of times but in fog it's a nightmare. Three cars were following each other when we came to some buildings. I got out to investigate. We'd only ended up in a farmyard.

Another time we'd been playing for a BOCM dance in Selby. There'd been a free buffet for the lads and again we came out to thick fog. Now the M62 had just been built and going up there was the first time any of us had travelled on it. We were returning in convoy, creeping along the motorway, when we realised we were travelling up the wrong side! We quickly made our way off and then stopped in a lay-by to get our bearings. Luckily, *Harry Bolder* had taken his instrument out of his case and filled it from the buffet, so we were able to calm our nerves with a good tuck in.

Norman smiled at the recollections. "Any more travelling stories?" I asked.

"Well we used to play for *Maisie Parkes* shows at The Beachomber in Cleethorpes and she would send a double decker bus to my little house in Auckland Avenue to pick up the gear. A single decker would come later to pick up the band as it was pre-bridge days and we had to go on the ferry. One trip Maisie returned on the bus with us and as usual she provided a crate of whisky and a crate of gin for the band. *Harry Bolder*, like the rest of us, had imbibed large quantities and when we arrived at the Parks residence asked if he could go to the loo before we carried on. He was pointed in the direction of the garages. Now Harry was wearing a brand new white mackintosh and just as he disappeared around a corner we heard an almighty crash and all rushed to investigate. He'd only fallen headfirst into a trough of oil. Not a white mac. any more. It was 6am before we arrived home and we were all at work that morning."

"I was once asked to play at a dance for Lord Hotham and I had to use a dep. As we were leaving, Lord Hotham was talking to a guest and this dep. shouted out: "Tara mister see ya agen sometime.' I could have died."

As I was talking to Norman I remembered a lovely tale from **Paul Shepherdson.** He said they'd been invited to do a gig in Malton. "Only one of us had a driving licence so we managed to get a horse box so we could all go together. It was a private party and we could have as much free booze as we wanted. Problem was the trumpeter had imbibed freely all-night and ended up collapsing in the middle of a set. He was unconscious. We finished the gig, then tried to revive him. We had to, he was the driver. We started off, but I'm afraid he drove straight though a prize orchard. We didn't get invited back."

But back to Norman. I asked him if he had any stories about punters.
"A couple. We always used to do a spot prize and I used to tell the dancers that the winner would be the man who brought me the sexiest underwear. One night in the middle of the dance floor, one guy dropped his pants. He was completely nude. Suffice to say he brought the house down so I just had to give him first prize.
"Another time we were playing at Beverley Road baths, when one of the instruments - probably **Roy Cooper's** trombone - caught an unsuspecting punter's wig. It shot off his head and landed beautifully on another dancer's left shoulder. Very embarrassing! But his face wasn't as red faced as the dancer who sneezed and his false teeth shot across the polished floor, coming to a halt in front of the band. He picked them up, then disappeared into the night."

Now some of the stories about Norman from his fellow musicians.

Eric Wright, his drummer, said he had given Norman two weeks notice to leave and relations between them were a bit strained. "He never spoke to me from the minute I gave in my notice. On the night before I was due to leave we had a gig at the Centre Hotel. In the interval the owner's dog had poohed under my seat. I told Norman but he wouldn't do anything about it so I headed for the licencee and told her to get someone to move it. 'Don't you dare speak to me like that,' she said, so I told her, 'If you don't get it moved the band goes on without a drummer. A few minutes later a porter came and shifted the stuff, telling me, 'my God, I don't know who's upset her, but she's in a sod of a mood.' At the end of the night she came railing up to Norman telling him, 'your band will never set foot in this place again,' Norman asked what was wrong and she pointed at me and said I'd insulted her. 'Don't worry' said Norman, 'I've sacked him!"

Eric smiled, "It gets better," he said. "A few weeks later, he desperately needed a drummer, but I'd gone out with my girl friend Eunice. Not many people could afford phones in those days, so he sent his wife Molly to my parents in East Hull and left a message asking if I'd play the following night as he couldn't get anybody. She had to catch two buses to get there. I said no chance so he ended up with *Jim Cleveland*, who normally played tenor, with a biscuit tin between his knees."

Norman accepted a two-week gig depping at the Locarno Ballroom, Bradford.
   "Don't worry," Norman told the musicians, "I'll arrange transport."
   "He did," said a band member. "A Pink Paraffin van."
   "Hey, don't knock it," said *Roy Cooper*, "that belonged to Herbert Smith, my father-in-law."
   His wife Heather continued. "Dad used to drive it all day, then rush home, swill it all out and nail boards at each side for the band to sit on. He would have a quick snack and then drive the band to Bradford. He absolutely loved every minute. But he told me he was terrified he left somebody behind, so every night he would count them all in and then count them all out."
   Now where have I heard that before?!
   Alf Stephenson interrupted. "Yes, but on the first night we got lost. Don't forget this was in the days before motorways and Bradford was a helluva way. We arrived an hour and a half late."
   "Ah, but we were dressed and ready to go on," said *Ray DesForges*."
   At that comment all the boys started laughing. *Dennis Proby* explained. "We had all come straight from work," he said, "so you can imagine the chaos as fifteen musicians tried to get changed into evening dress, in a bloody van!"
   Which made Heather ask Ray if he remembered the night he had to nurse her two year old daughter Lynn all the way to Bradford. "How we all squeezed

in I'll never know, because of course there were all the instruments as well. My brother Paul, who used to pack them, had it off to a fine art."

Heather also told me that the van had her Dad's telephone number on the side, "It was amazing how many jobs he got in the West Riding."

"What I remember," said *Ray DesForges* is that one night all the electric's' on the van failed on our way home. And Herbert rang the Electricity Board to come and help. They bloody did, but we didn't get home until 4.30am and I was getting married at eleven!" He turned to Heather. "It's been bugging me all these years. Why did your dad ring up the electricity board?"

"Simple," said Heather," he worked for them part-time and knew one of the lads was a dab hand with car's electric's'."

"I knew there must have been a sensible answer," said Ray.

"What I remember about those trips," said *Roy Cooper*, "is that nobody was allowed to light a cigarette, for obvious reasons and the lads complained all the way, because of course everybody smoked in those days."

Bradford, Locarno obviously brought back many fond memories.

The *Norman Mail Big Band* also depped for two weeks at Hull's Locarno ballroom. *Ray DesForges* recalled: " It was a revolving stage and we were rehearsing on the Sunday morning and were at the back practising playing as the stage revolved. Norman pressed the button for the stage to start moving, except the tower holding the bingo balls hadn't been cleared from the night before and the top hit a gantry, toppling it to the floor. We were picking up bingo balls for hours."

While playing at the Beverley Road Baths, the boys were all in for a shock. Norman had arranged with *Les Robertson* to sort out the pad. As the boys started playing they found that on every second sheet, a photograph of a very glamorous female was looking up at them, completely naked!

Norman was renowned for stamping very forcibly with his right foot. So hard in fact, that during a gig at Withernsea Pavilion, the manager came and asked him not to stamp so loudly. Evidently the floor was hollow and the noise was horrific in the dressing rooms below. Norman tried, but the acts waiting in the dressing rooms below, were still complaining, so the manager made everybody happy by putting a pillow under that offending right foot.

Tony Richards said he was taking lessons from *Noel Flint* when Norman rang to ask if he could play for him. "I explained I'd never played ith a band and was still learning, but he said to help me out he would let me play for the experience but not pay me. Noel wasn't very happy but I accepted and I think I did about four gigs before I got paid, but it was a great experience."

No one is excempt from being the butt of musician's jokes and Norman was no exception.

They are renowned for their one-liners. Norman had a car accident and turned up at the gig with his leg in plaster. Immediate comment from the boys. 'Oh God Norman, you're not going to have to play with your hands tonight are you?"

Sorry Norman.

Some of the personnel who played for Norman included:
Piano: *Norman Mail*. Bass: *Noel Flint, Tony Richards,* Drums: *Paul Shepherdson. Eric Wright.*
Trumpets; *Alf Stephenson, Les Robertson, Keith Parker, Harry Bolder*
Saxophones: *Dennis Proby* (Alto) *Ray DesForges* and *Jim Cleveland* (tenor)
Trombones: *Roy Cooper*

LEN MANLEY

Len was not resident at a particular venue but was a well-known 'gig' band.

He had a huge library of Old Tyme dances, but when he died he'd left instructions that the whole library should be destroyed.

"He was a stickler for good manners, said *Frank Cleveland*. "He would never let you call him by his first name it always had to be Mr Manley. I remember my first gig with him, the muso's were all in evening dress but the punters were all in tails and the men were all wearing white gloves."

He suddenly remembered, "*Kenny Baker* played with him, also *Harry Chatterton*. Frank told me that if they were playing at a dinner dance, he would insist on the musicians having a proper meal in the restaurant with the diners.

"We'd arrived one night and our meal was in a buffet style in another room. Len insisted they set tables for the musicians with the other diners. "If you don't, you'll have no musicians and no musicians means you don't have a dance."

Trevor Hickson also played for the band. "His pad was immaculate," said Trevor. "Every number was already in the order it was to be played on your stand and we never, ever deviated."

GENE MAYO

This was a professional band that played at the Locarno Ballroom. *Maisie Parkes* was presenting a special show, a well known figure in the area and the band had to be augmented for the occasion. Gene had arranged a rehearsal on the Sunday morning, but *George Wilcox* had hurt his back and was unable to play, so asked *Ray DesForges* to dep. for him. Gene was the band 'wit' and took badly to anyone upstaging him, he also liked a tipple or two. While the band were looking for dots or sorting their pad, Gene would suriptiously nip off stage and have a quick swig. He had just made another 'entrance' with an armful of sheet music when he tripped and the lot went flying. Ray made a jest, which did not go down well with Mr Mayo. "If you were in my band you'd be bloody fired."

"I wouldn't mind," said Ray, "But I had a bad back as well and was only doing it as a favour to George." *Noel Flint* told him,"You must be the only musician to be sacked from a rehearsal."

John Mallinder (Alto) said that *Fred Ashworth* sliced his finger on the cymbals. "Blood spurted out everywhere. He grabbed his hankie from his jacket pocket, wrapped it tightly around the wound and played on. We managed to get it sorted out in the interval," said John, "but it was a pretty bad cut."

The boys were not letting him off easily. "I know you think you're a bloody good drummer, but there's no need to go to those lengths to prove it Fred."

Keith Parker said he was read to go on stage one night when his trouser zip went. "Not a pretty sight," said Keith, "so I quickly whipped them off and put them on back to front. I wouldn't mind but they were about ten years old and were so shiny, they reflected like silver in the lights. They were very uncomfortable but an improvement on letting the punters see my Pink Panther underpants!"

I was also told about a dep. who never warmed his tenor up before going on stage. "We were all sat in position ready to start as the revolving stage started spinning. Dennis never made a sound. He'd forgotten to put a reed in!"

Line-up: Bass: *Noel Flint* Drums: *Fred Ashworth*
Trumpets: *Rose Hargeaves, Keith Parker, Pete Dawson*
Trombone: *Eddie Hargreaves*
Sax's: *John Mallinder, George Wilcox*
Vocals: *Donny Keith*
Guitar: *Bill Brown.*

THE NEW YORKERS

Formed in November 1945, playing nightly they soon established themselves, gathering a tremendous following:
    Lineup: Saxophones: *Alf. Thorpe, Reg. Bates, Stan Grey, Johnny Franklin.*
    Trumpets: *George Footitt, George Mather, Frank Cocking, Billy Clutterbrook.*
    Trombones: *Harry Robb, Alan Smith, Percy Stather, Horace Holloway.*
    Rhythm - Piano: *Bill Edkins.* Drums: *Cyril Sellars* Bass: *Frank Wignall*
    Spanish Guitar: *Arthur Bryant.*

GRAHAM PINKNEY SHOW BAND

I feel should include this band as so many local musicians played in it. It was based at the Wallis's Holiday Camp at Cayton Bay.
    Every week they introduced a celebrity of the time. They were interviewed by Graham on stage. They included. *Alexandra Bastedo, Betty Driver, David Hamilton, Hughie Green, Jean Alexandra, Monica Rose* and *Liz Dawn* (Vera Duckworth in Coronation Street, said she started her career, in a talent contest at the camp.

She then went on to appear at many working men's clubs. She recalled one fateful night at a west Yorkshire venue. "I was followed by Cannon and Ball," she said, "But was not going very well, so I told them, 'look nobodies listening so I might as well as go.' A man shouted, 'Well f*** off then,' so I did. Then the manager came and told me off for insulting his customers!"

Graham is a multi-instrumentalist, who started young. His parents, who ran a guesthouse in Bridlington, bought him a xylophone for his fourth birthday and one day there was a great commotion when they found little Graham had gone missing. Everyone was called in to search for him. Nearly two hours had passed and his parents were just calling for the police when some guests spotted him on the promenade. There was a small crowd listening intently to him showing his skills on his new toy. They showed their appreciation by showering him with money, unaware of the furore he had left behind.

He continued to try out various instruments and by the tender age of thirteen was asked to play for *Ceres Harper* in the Promenade Cafe. He had to take his drum kit to the gig in a wheelbarrow. He left school at sixteen as he was offered a summer season at the Spa Theatre, Bridlington. He told me. "I was earning considerably more than my father, who was a senior electrical engineer."

He also recalled a time, while in the RAF.

"We were on morning parade and it was freezing. There we were all lined up and the band marched onto the parade ground. I was a 'back marker' playing bass. I was giving it some wellie when I suddenly realised I couldn't hear the rest of the band. I peeked over my instrument and realised I was alone. I'd bloody missed the left wheel order hadn't I? It took a long time for me to live that one down!"

The Show Band in Scarborough consisted of fifteen musicians and played for six nights a week. The Hull boys took it in turn to drive, well all except *Brian Hargrave*. He was always a passenger because a normal nights intake for him was ten pints and he was always complaining, "I don't know where my money goes, it's coming to a fine mess when I can't afford the intervals."

Brian is fondly known as 'Snuffy'. This nickname came about after the boys had been to a *Jimmy James* show. On stage the dialogue went something like this.

"Ely, 'as he been in?"

"Has who been in?"

"Ely. *Snuffy Hargraves*."

So there it was, **Brian Hargrave,** trumpeter, was instantly saddled with 'Snuffy.'

All the musicians had a tale to tell me about him. Evidently his timekeeping is legendary. Whatever time they had to collect him, the boys would make it half-an-hour earlier but he was still never ready. As you went in the door, you could hear the plaintive cry. "Me socks, I've lost me socks?"

They'd set off one night, late as usual, when **Paul Gibbins** said. "I didn't see your trumpet Snuffy"

"Oh my God, exploded Brian, "It's in the boot of my car."

"And where's your car?"

"Safeways, it's gone shopping with the wife."

Returning home he invariably fell asleep before anyone else. It was instant. On one occasion he was heard to mutter, "I could murder a..." and silence. He was fast asleep. As they hit Beverley, about a mile from his home, he suddenly jerked forward and proclaimed, "... a vindaloo."

They were discussing a personality who'd died and Brian asked "Is he HMV positive?" As the deceased was a singer, they all thought this highly appropriate.

Another occasion one of the boys had farted and Brian made a great fuss about the smell and opened the electronically operated window to get some fresh air. He leant partly out of the window and inadvertently leant on the control button and up the window went, trapping his hair. He was screaming "Help me, help me, me hair hurts," but the passengers were too busy having hysterics beside him.

If he didn't fall asleep, he never stopped talking. The two in the back with him always pretended to be asleep. When Brian is in talking mode, he flits from subject to subject without taking breath. I asked for a typical conversation:

"I used to have a fairisle jumper. Me dad worked on the trains and I can still smell oily rags. I don't like them without sleeves though. (Looking out the window, but still not pausing for breath) Look at that, it reminds me of when I was young. I like the moon. I always got a comic with a moon on it."

If he was aware of anyone falling asleep, he would poke them in the chest and tell them,"I'm being serious now."

I was also told: "Snuffy drove a battered, rusty old Vauxhall with no interior trim. It was known by all the muso's as the 'Snufmobile'."

One night a party was planned after the show and **Roy Cooper** rang his wife Heather to come and pick him up. "But I'd rolled the car into a ditch," said Heather. "The camp manager brought Roy to me. There I was standing at the side of the road when Roy jumped out of the car and ran towards me. His first words? 'I hope my trombones all right."

The next day **Alf Stephenson** took us to the car, then arranged for a local farmer to pull us out with a tractor."

Alf seemed to spend half his life rescuing musicians from ditches. *Ray DesForges* recalled the time he'd pulled him from a ditch at Weel.

I asked how it got there in the first place, but all I got were two cheeky grins.

During an interval at Wallis's Holiday camp, one of the musicians (I was under pain of death not to even mention the instrument!) had gone back to the dressing room with a 'Player Personality' girl. These were a posse of pretty girls who were there to promote Players cigarettes. The rest of the band were in the bar, or so they thought, when they heard somebody trying the door handle, but the door had been locked. It was the drummer returning to get something from his bag. He started banging on the door. "What's going on in there?" The two recalcitrants flung their clothes back on and opened the door. "Oops, sorry," said the drummer, realising what had been happening. The embarrassed girl rushed out and the drummer apologised again. "Its too bloody late now isn't it?" said the musician and started to wriggle uncomfortably, then proceeded to take his pants off.

"Its my underpants," said the musician, "I've put them on back to front."

"That's what they call screwing up your arrangements," said the drummer.

Line-up for the Graham Pinkney Showband.
Organ/vibes/xylophone/drums/trombone *Graham Pinkney*
Lead trumpet/flugal horn/valve trombone: *Alf Stephenson, Brian Hargrave, Alan Cross.*

Piano/organ/ *Bill Edkins* (Tues/Sat)
Piano/organ (wed/thurs.fri/sat) *Phillip Honner*
Sax's: *John Mallinder, Len Rangely, Dennis Proby, Mick Richardson, Ray DesForges*
Trombone: *Harry Chatterton, John Hardy, Roy Cooper.*
Bass guitar: *Ken Cook*
Guitar: *Roy Chilton*
Drums/percussion: *Dave Pinkney*
Vocalist: *Richard Rodgers.*
With the exception of the rhythm section and the vocalist all the band members travelled from Hull every night.

Roy Cooper decided that instead of travelling to and from the venue, he would hire a small caravan on site for himself, wife and baby. His wife Heather took up the tale. "And we had a boxer dog in there as well," she told me. "How big was the van?" I asked. She smiled. "It was one of those small round ones, about fourteen foot long and would you believe nearly every night, all the band used to come in for a party. The thing had no electricity and one gas lamp for lighting."

"That sounds fun!"

"Oh we didn't mind, but a lot of them were spilling out onto the grass and they used to stop for hours sometimes. One night there was a commotion and lots of shouting. Then I heard, 'There's a bloody sheep in here.' How it'd managed to squeeze through that lot without anyone saying anything, I'll never know. But we were having a good time! Trouble was I'd got a job in one of the kiosks and had to be up quite early but it worked quite well really. Roy would look after the baby during the day and when he was working, it was my turn. I think Lynn enjoyed all the attention."

"And the dog loved it as well," added Roy.

"Not as much as we enjoyed having him," giggled Heather. "We have a secret. He found the butcher's shop on the camp and used to come home with some very succulent cuts of meat. Perfect for a hard up musician."

Ray DesForges showed me a programme from 1970, so I could check dates and line-up, but he had obviously forgotten a note scribbled on the front. 'I'll love you forever. Kathleen.'

I wonder where Kathleen is now?

LESLIE ROSE

He advertised as 'any combination'.

Les was originally at Withernsea Pavilion, then went on to the Beverly Road Baths. In 1953 he became resident at Hull's City Hall, notching up a formidable ten years.

All of the musicians who played in the **Les Rose Orchestra** said, they enjoyed playing with Les because "It was such a bloody good laugh."

The band were all confirmed gigglers and leading the merrymakers seemed to be **Frankie (Wiggy) Wade** - Bass.

"It was not unusual to see him standing there wearing false ears. He also had a glass of imitation beer beside him and pretended to swig out of it all night.

At a certain passage in the number, 'Chick-a-Biddy, ' Wiggy would play below the bridge, making an indescribable noise which set the band off."

"What sort of noise?"

"Very, very high, a sort of Ricky tick-tick." It got to the point when we knew it was coming, the brass would collapse in anticipation. Tommy Sykes would be in such a state his glasses would steam up."

Jack Barker said, "All you could see was the shoulders of the sax section heaving and in the end Les got so fed up he refused to play the number anymore. We all played tricks on each other. Poor old Ray Des. had a rough time, everytime he got up to play, a trombonist would put a mute on his chair."

"As a band leader I had to have some decorum," said Les, "but when Ray Des blew, he always puffed his cheeks out, so whenever I turned and caught sight of him, it invariably 'corpsed me.'"

Alf Stephenson recalls: "*Jack Barker* and myself both had some false teeth on a palette and they would suddenly start to slip, so at various times they had to be 'fixed' with powder. As we shot off stage I would mutter, ' its okay lads I'm just going for a quick fix.' Quite a different connotation today," commented Alf.

Saturday nights at the City Hall were often attended by the wives of **Les Horncastle, Jack Barker** and **Doug Sewell**, sometimes accompanied by Les

Rose's wife. They always sat on the right of the balcony, which all the boys dubbed, 'The Royal Box.'

Tommy Sykes suffered a great deal from cold sores. "It was not unusual to see blood streaming from his lips. In fact they were so painful, he couldn't take his instrument from his lips."

In the summer you could guarantee that *Doug Sewell* would arrive at the last minute still dressed in his whites from a cricket match.

The personnel used included:

Keyboards: *Ray Hammond, Reg. Cook*, Bass: *Frank (Wiggy) Wade, Dave Walker.*

Drums: *Johnny Franks.*

Trumpets: *Jack Barker, Tommy Sykes, Keith Parker,*

Trombones: *Arthur Norris, John Hardy.*

Saxes: *Leslie Rose, Ray DesForges, Dougie Sewell, Peter Bellamy, Les Horncastle, George Appleyard, Dave Wilson, Ray Scott.*

COLIN SHAKESPEARE

Colin was resident at Hornsea Floral hall for several years having taken over from *Eric Williams*. He also gigged around the Hull area with a big band.

I asked where he got most of his experience. "In the forces really." He smiled. "But I had a really useful dodge. When the squad was asked if anyone played an instrument, I would own up to being a saxophone player, but that the instrument was at home, which was Willerby Rd., Hull. In no time at all I was in the possession of a weekend pass and travel warrant to collect the instrument. It worked every time.

He continued: "I was stationed in the Middle East and had the temerity to write and ask the 'Middle East Command Dance Band (based in Cairo) for an audition. The band was made up solely of professional musicians who had been called up for active service.

For the audition I was asked to play alto. The pad was chock-a-block full of original arrangements and I'd never seen manuscript hand written before, let alone tried to play one. I soon realised I was way out of his league, but they were nice chaps and realising my inexperience let me down gently. My pride was hurt, but it was a classic case of 'don't ring me, I'll ring you."

"Any stories about the band?"

"Not really, but I don't know if you know but **Frank Ayers**, my drummer, used to repair all brass instruments as well as drums and although his grand-daughter Karen doesn't play, she now also repairs woodwind instruments."

I asked Colin if he also gave lessons like so many of the musicians. He admitted he did. "But today's exams are completely different and it's pleasing that examination boards are becoming much more tolerant of jazz."

Later in the day I was talking to **Jim Lundy**, his vocalist. "I have a story you might like. Nothing to do with Colin's band though."

"Carry on, the floor's yours."

"Well for years I was the manager of a wine shop in a pretty suburban area of Hull.

It was Monday lunchtime and I'd left the door open in the shop as it was excessively hot. I was on the phone and didn't hear anyone enter. As I turned, at the counter was a regular customer. A very attractive, well educated lady, about forty-five years old. She was always dressed immaculately. This time she was wearing a white lace blouse, which accentuated her tan. We made small talk as I processed her order. She picked up the carrier, containing her drink and stood back a pace or two, while continuing the conversation. She was now in full view. And I mean full! She had forgotten to put a skirt on and I was faced with a black triangle staring at me. My brain eventually came out of neutral and I could see the headlines, in the Hull Daily Mail. 'Local man takes, wine, women and song, literally.' - She played the tenor saxophone, but more than that I will not go - any minute now the shop would be over-run with school children, wanting their cans of coke and crisps.

I coughed and mumbled and repeated my 'byes' and she turned to go, giving me another perspective of her ample charms. As she reached the door, she turned again to talk to me, her 'derrie-air' on full view to any passing pedestrian. This happened to be a nineteen year old, male bank employee. I swear I saw smoke coming from his shoes as he skidded to a halt. He gave me a cursory wave and shot back from whence he came. The lady was already turning to go. She climbed into her car, parked outside and with a cheery wave, drove off.

I saw her on numerous occasions after that, but I daren't broach the subject and she always carried on as normal. The bank clerk came in the next day and asked me how I did it at my age!"

Personnel included: Piano: *Eric Williams*. Bass: *Martin Shaw, Dennis Aylwin.*
Drums: *Frank Ayers.*
Tenor: *Mick Richardson, Lennie Rangely.* Alto: *Colin Shakespeare.*
Trumpet: *Alf Stephenson, Keith Parker, Wally Ingram, Brian Hargrave.*
Vocalist: *Jim Lundy.*

The Les Rose Orchestra at the City Hall

Part of the Sax. Section, Leslie Rose Orchestra, Beverley Road Baths, 1958
L/R: Ray Desforges, Les Horncastle, Doug Sewell - Bass: Frank (Wiggy) Wade

Jim Lundy rehearsing with The Colin Shakepseare Band

Part of the Colin Shakespeare Band
Front Row L/R" Noel Weston, Colin Shakespeare, Len Rangely

Norman Mail Band, Locarno Ballrom, Hull

Norman Mail Band - Vocalist: Ray Desforges

Graham Pinkney Showband 1970

Wallis's 1985
L/R: Len Rangely, Sheila Edkins, Freddy Adamson, Julie Edkins, Graham Pinkney

Norman Mail Band, Blind Institute
L/R: Harry Bolder, Mick Richardson, Pete Bellamy, Jim Cleveland, Tony Richards,
Wally Oaten

The Gene Mayo Orchestra

SIOUX CITY SEVEN (Skiffle group)

Not one of your strict tempo bands but the group started playing at the Bricknell Avenue Methodist Youth Club in uniforms of white shirts, blacks trousers and bow-tie. Well it was 1957.

The leader of the group *Paul Sheperdson* said: "We started with a lot of opposition, but we soon managed to get a good following. People would jive non-stop for two hours at a time. It got really wild at times. We also had a fifteen year old schoolgirl, Kay Bulliegh, as our vocalist, but *Alan Hirst* pinched her from me. She eventually changed her name to *Kay Garner*."

Paul went on to play for several bands as well forming his own. He recalls a gig in Sheffield. "When we got there we found seven hundred fellah's all baying for the strippers. The chairman was 80 if he was a day, with the mandatory flat cap and bell. 'Can we 'ave a bit of quiet,' only meant more raucous yelling. We'd done about four numbers and he told us to get off. 'They don't like you,' he told us, 'so you needn't bother to come back.' He paid us ten bob (.50p) for the night - not each, that's for the whole band, then as we were going home we got a puncture. That cost me ten shillings. So with the cost of the drinks and petrol, it had cost us money to do the gig."

He also recalled *Fred Yeadon, Ken Ford* and *Andy Peacock* organising an 'exchange' visit to France. "Fred was a pretty heavy drinker and was usually first one in the pub. The first gig was in the Town Hall, full of local dignitaries. Fred was so drunk by the time they were due to start, the others had to lead him in, sit him on the stool and place his hands on the keys. We took turns at nudging him to keep awake and secondly so he didn't stop playing."

"Talking about sleeping, I remember the drummer *Roy Wilkin* would always like a nap on his way home. A couple of times I passed a lay-by only to see his car parked up, but it's not what you think. His wife used to travel with him. She was not amused."

He smiled. "Then there was the trumpeter *Derek Lorrison*. He caused a real problem for the rhythm section. If he couldn't reach a note he wanted, he would go as high as he could then change key corresponding to the note he wanted to reach. Oh and there was the time *Gordon Findlay* was playing his socks off when he suddenly tipped right off the end of his stool.

"We also had a trombone player who could drink anyone under the table, but one night we'd just completed the Last waltz and he literally fell off his chair onto the floor, where he stayed. He was fast asleep!

"There was another trombone player who depped for us and as he walked on stage we noticed he had no shoes. 'It's all right,' he told us, 'I make such a racket stamping my foot that I have to take my shoes off.'

"What about Mr Shepherdson the band leader?"
He grinned mischievously.
"Me? I was always the epitome of decorum. Mind you sometime in 1960 I was playing in Blackpool and my tom-tom fell off and booled loudly down the raked stage. I had to get up and walk down to pick the thing up. I got a great cheer from the audience but the band leader was not impressed."

SOUNDS EASY

A seven piece, resident at the Grange Park Hotel, reviving the music from the 'Good Old Days' and bringing back the dance band sound to our area.

"One night while playing for the diners," said *Paul Gibbins*, "We suddenly realised the portable dance floor was slowly shuffling forward on top of the newly laid carpet, eventually pinning the band to the wall. The manager was called at the interval and he arranged for the floor to be returned to its original position and wedges of wood to be placed against the wall to prevent it from creeping any further. After the interval *Ray DesForges* announced to the audience. 'That must be the first time Wedgwood has been used to block the stage.' His attempts at a gag, fell on deaf ears. I told him I thought it was funny."

"We had a gig at a prestigious event in Sheffield," said *Johnny Mallinder*, "and normally *Ray DesForges* took all the gear as he stored it in his garage, but this time **Paul (Gibbins)** offered to take it on his trailer, leaving space for three musicians in Ray's car. We arrived at the venue and Paul was waiting at the door for us. 'Have you already set up?' we asked.'"
"What are you taking about? You've got the gear."

"No, you said you were bringing it on the trailer."

Despite four witnesses to the fact, he was not convinced he'd ever made the offer. 'Don't worry,' said Paul, 'I'll ring Pat (his wife). He did and with the help of their teenage son, the trailer was loaded up with the amplifiers and driven to Sheffield.

"How did you explain that to the punters?"

"We didn't have to. Pat arrived with nearly twenty minutes to spare, so by the time we'd set up, we were spot on."

"Later that night *Eric* (*Seaward*) had been unaware that his chair had been slowly shuffling backward. Suddenly Eric and chair fell three feet over the edge of the stage.

Nobody took much notice, he just climbed back on and continued playing. He did get a small cheer from the audience.

"He wasn't hurt then?"

"I suppose you could say he was shaken but not stirred," said a band member.

"A bit like his playing really," said another.

They were also the backing band for the *Joe Loss* at the Spa Theatre Bridlington and the audience was queuing up for an hour before the doors opened.

Keith Parker commented, "All the old familiar faces were dancing past. It was like going back in time thirty years."

Personnel: Piano: *Eric Seaward*. Drums: *Dave Harvey*. Bass: *Paul Gibbins*.
Sax's: *John Mallinder* (Alto) *Ray DesForges* (tenor and vocals)
Trumpet: *Keith Parker*.
The female vocals were ably performed by *Brenda Wood*.

Just thought you might like to know. The bass player *Paul Gibbins* is the son of the well known band leader *Ambrose Gibbins*.

THREE BLIND MICE

This group cropped up a couple of times in conversations with musicians. It was thought the name came about because they were all blind. It was suggested they were resident at Reckitt and Coleman, but it was not certain so I put out a plea for more information in **Rex. Booth's Flashback** column in the Hull Daily Mail, but no one came forward to help.

NORRIS WALKER

The band was well known for being, "a very friendly lot and Norris was always impeccably turned out, plus they were a very good dance band."

Doris Harland recalls: "in the band there were three George's and they all had moustaches, as did Norris. He had a cycle shop on Cottingham Road, opposite the Goodfellowship Inn and he used to take part in T.T races in Ireland.

"I used to sing ballads like 'Falling Leaves' and those sort of oldies. We would sing twenty songs a night for twenty-five shillings. (£1.25) but you had to be in the Musician's Union.

I particularly remember when we played at the Hull Fair dance. We were up on the balcony and the lady dancers were in crinolines. It was so spectacular. Don't forget this was in the late 40's."

Eric Wright took over from *Pat Cornell* on drums and on his first gig he said: "This guy came up to me, with a suitcase in one hand and a tenor in the other. 'Hi,' he said, 'I'm *Jim* (*Carlill*) how many do you want?'"
"How many what?"
"Bottles."
"Bottles of what?"
"Beer. Pat always had three."
"Well I'd better have three as well. That started me off, I'd never had a drink in my life before that." He laughed. "He even provided us with a plastic beaker as well."

Frank Cleveland said: "One night when *Joan Richardson* (Jo. Peters) got up to sing, *Clarrie Baynton,* a big tall fellah, who always carried his instrument in an old kitbag, put a whoopie cushion on her chair and when she sat back down, the noise was horrendous. Norris went ballistic. I think that's the only time I saw him in a real temper. He said I don't mind you messing about amongst yourselves, but leave Jo. out of your childish pranks. Trouble was Joanne thought it hilarious."

"The first ever gig I did with did with *Norris Walker* was at the City Hall," said *Eric Wright.* "We were playing away when suddenly there was this almighty crash when *Harry Robb,* leant backwards in his chair and the whole thing toppled over. Chair, music, trombone and Harry crashed to the ground. He scrabbled around for a while then sorted himself out and carried on. Norris never even glanced his way, he just kept on playing."

He is remembered fondly by the musicians as a 'gent'. *Joanne Richardson* was his regular vocalist and for months she wondered what was going on when Norris said, 'Right boys, washleathers'.
"It was ages before I realised he was telling them they could go for a pee, but he didn't like saying it front a lady."

As in all bands they sometimes have to call in a dep. and band jackets were a problem. "You can bet your bottom dollar," said Joanne, "that the short fat trumpeter would be replaced by a six-foot three barber's pole, or the other way round. I don't know which was funnier, the bean-pole wearing a 46 inch chest, with sleeves finishing at his elbows, or the short, very fat musician trying to manoeuvre his ample frame into the 36 inch."

Another story told to me by *John Carnazza,* about that infamous road to Withernsea. "We were all in convoy, led by *Harry Robb* on his motorbike and sidecar. As you know it's a perilous road, full of bends," explained John. "Well Harry took a corner a bit fast and shot through a gate into a field, turning the bike over. Nobody was hurt so we helped get the bike on the road again. Except it was like a quagmire, one that had been invaded by cows, and we were all in evening dress. We had gunk up to our knees and I'm afraid went on the stand in that condition."

I asked John how he started playing and he told me he had been accepted for the Royal College with piano as his first instrument and clarinet as his second. "I hadn't been at college long when I knew I wouldn't get many gigs in Hull playing the clarinet, so I thought about it and realised double bass players were a bit thin on the ground. So that made my mind up for me."

"Did you go straight into a band?"

"Well sort of. My cousin Clive, a drummer, who ran a band at the Majestic Ballroom in Leeds, had accepted an invitation to play on board a boat, so I'd taken him to the docks and was very impressed. Don't forget I was only 24. Anyway I got myself a job on the Union Castle sailing to South Africa. Loved every minute. Then when I returned, went to play with Norris."

John is one of the few musicians who are no longer playing, so I asked him what he'd done wirh his instrument, as double basses are probably only seen in jazz clubs now.

"Funny you should ask that, but it was only a couple of months ago I got the courage up to part with it. I didn't know anyone locally who might want it, so I put it up for auction."

Personnel included: Keyboard/Band leader: **Norris Walker.**
Bass: **John Carnazza. Jack Rudd.**
Drums: **Pat Cornell. Eric Wright.**
Tenor: **Jimmy Carlill.** Alto: **George Spicer.**
Trombone: **Harry Robb**
Trumpet: **Ernie Stewart. Arthur Asquith.**
Bass: **Jack Rudd.**
Vocals: **Doris Harland, Joanne Richardson.**

THE ERIC WRIGHT TRIO

Eric played for several seasons at Cave Castle in South Cave with **Gordon Findlay** on piano and **Len Dodsworth** on Bass.

THE WHITE HOUSE 'SWINGTETTE'

A group that played nightly at this venue, an advert of the time told us it was a: 'A snappy Combination that offers the exclusive type of night-life music that fits the mood of the diner and the dancer.'

Pianist/Band leader: *Arthur Gibbins*. Drums/Vibraphone: *Jack Lee*.
Bass: *Jimmy Stewart*
Sax/clarinet: *Fred Rawson*.

Sioux City Seven 1958

Trevor Hickson with Hughie Green when he won Opportunity Knocks at the Phoenix Club

L/R: Brenda Fountain, Paul Gibbins, Ray Desforges, John Mallinder, Keith Parker

Eric Wright Trio, Duke of Cumberlain 1970
L/R: Gordon Findlay, Dennis Aylwin, Eric Wright

Walton Street 1975
L/R: Mick Richardson, Len Rangely

L/R: Eric Wright, Bert Boots, Sheila Kinsey, Bill Kinsey 1958

Alf Stephenson fronting Jazz Vehicle

Frank Cleveland

Vocalist Jean Longbottom in the outfit she wore at the Christmas and New Year Festivities at the White House and New York Hotel 1958

Band Leader: Bill Kinsey

Piano: Bill Kinsey - Bass: Bill Pickles - Drums: Bert Hickey - Trumpet: Tony Dobson

Trevor Hickson

The Newington Orchestra

THE RISE AND FALL OF THE BALLROOM

ADELAIDE CLUB , Hessle Road

I have included this venue because so many of the musicians went to have a blow. It didn't cater for dancing, only cabaret acts, But it had a reputation of attraction top musicians from the area and you could guarantee a full house.

John Carnazza said it a bit like a hole in the ground. The roofs leaked so badly, when it rained, they put buckets out to catch the water. Also the ceiling was so low, you couldn't see across the roof some night, as don't forget this was in the 1950's and nearly everybody smoked in those days."

I asked him who played regularly at the club and he recalled: "Well I was on bass, *Eric Smith* on piano, he really was a brilliant pianist, then we had *Ev Snowden* on clarinet and *Billy Clutterbrook* on trumpet. *Leon Riley* used to do a few vocals for us and a guy called *Sammy Walsham* was the MC."

John then suddenly remembered a vocalist called *Alan Bell* who sometimes joined them." We made him welcome - then we found out he was a tax man."

ASSEMBLY ROOMS - Victoria Square

The *Ken Brookes Band* held the residency. *Frank Cleveland* said he always came with a crate of beer. "Very popular with the musicians."

You can still see pictures and some posters in a nearby cafè.

BEVERLEY ROAD BATHS

During the winter months the pools were drained and a hardwood floor laid over them.

The roof and the balcony were draped with coloured fabric and subdued lighting was installed to add to the atmosphere.

Because it consisted of two rooms it could cater for all sizes of audience. M.C's in attendance were *S. Nellist* and *A. Carmichael*. Spot prizes were numerous throughout the evening. Admittance was 10/6. (52p) Buses would be queuing up to take the dancers home.

Normally *Tommy Fisher*, with his wife, *Peggy Edwards*, as vocalist would play in the small baths. One musician told me, "Peggy really felt the cold. I don't ever remember seeing her without a cardigan." In the 'big baths' the dancers usually whirled the night away to the *Norris Walker Band*.

All the big firms in Hull had their annual dances at Beverley Road Baths. The musicians still fondly recall the nights they played for the Hull Judeans, Fishmongers, Wholesale Fruit Merchants, Humber Street, Hull Daily Mail and of course the Musician's Union Ball when eight bands from Hull were given a chance to show their paces. The musicians gave their services free for the benefit of the Musician Union's benevolent fund.

I found a cutting that quoted the line-up for one evening as follows:

Small stage: *Alf Taylor - Al Jenner - The Adelaides - Harry Chatterton*
Main Stage: *Tommy Fisher - Leslie Rose - Eddie Bentley - Teddy Barker*.

Frank and *Ricky Cleveland* told me. "In those days we often left our instruments underneath the stage for the next gig, certain they wouldn't be nicked."

Leslie Rose and *Maxwell Daniels* always fronted the Hull Judeans Dance and the bands always had the same compliment of musicians. One year Max found Les had a player more than him, so asked the band if they knew anyone who could sit in. *Len Rangely* told him, "*Ray DesForges* plays tenor and he's in the audience. He was approached and was delighted as he was still a novice

-although his girl friend **Maureen Bilton** wasn't so pleased - Luckily he only lived a mile away, so ran all the way home, returning in half-an-hour with his instrument. A chair had been placed in the front ready for him. The music stand was empty. 'Where's the dots?" asked Ray.

"You haven't got any," replied Max. "I just want you to make as if you're playing. I spent the whole evening miming, but best of all I got paid," said Ray, "and it got better. A few weeks later **Tommy Sykes** contacted me to say **Les. Rose** needed a replacement as **George Appleyard** was leaving. Excellent timing," said Ray, "It was the perfect introduction to a top class band."

The majority of dancers came by bus and when everyone spilled out after the dance, there would usually be four buses lined up along Beverley Road, two facing town and two facing Beverley. They were usually pre-booked at the dance and cost approx. 6p. The bus took a circuitous route and you just rang the bell when you wanted get off.

Many musicians joined them, except those that had travelled to the gig by bike. The idea of a drummer or string bass travelling by either mode of transport is quite mind-boggling. But they thought nothing of it. Fred told me, "It was tricky stacking drums under the stairs and you wouldn't believe the times the bloody things got stuck. Most of us had to change buses at Paragon Station and had difficulty retrieving our kit. The conductors usually helped drag it out, but woe betide the musician if the bus was running late. They were threatened with, "Look I've got a schedule to keep. If you don't get it off my bus, we leave the bloody lot there." and as one discerning conductor said, "Why do you have to bring so many?"

One band arriving early found the baths locked up, they eventually managed to alert someone and asked if they could let them in.
"I don't know you from Adam."
"He's outside bringing in the gear."
"Oh all right then."

Speaking to some of the regulars, I was told you weren't allowed to drink alcohol at Beverley Road Baths. Frank recalled "My friend and I would smuggle some beer in and sneak to the loos to drink it, but there was a security man who was up to many of the lads tricks. One Saturday we'd just gone to the lav's to have a drink when we heard him coming. 'Quick stick it in a cistern' said my friend. The security guy arrived and there we were peeing happily. 'Don't worry lads,' he said, 'I'm just looking for any booze. Some of these lads think they can get the better of me,' and with that he started to examine the cisterns and sure enough found our four bottles of illicit booze. 'There you are what did I tell you?' he announced. 'Tell you what lads, let's share it. That'll show them.' So there we were having to share our own beer."

I think the piéce de résistance for this venue must be the time over 300 people danced to Louis Armstrong and his famous Harlem Band, which were appearing at the Tivoli Theatre. "The occasion was Civic Week Staff Dance organised by Mr Sidney Scarborough. Among those present was Mr Broadbent, a representative of the Marconi Phone Company who is visiting Hull in connection with the big amplifier loaned to the Corporation for Civic Week Functions". The date? Thursday 12th Oct. 1933. The cost? 3/6 (17$\frac{1}{2}$p)

A visit by Louis Armstrong took place in October 1933. The press report stated: "He has lips of iron yet supple as rubber, producing wonderful high notes. He was producing top E natural without effort.

BEVIN HOUSE (Farmery Hall) George St. Hull

Advertised as; 'Hull's Most Luxurious Ballroom.'

B.P always held their staff dances at Bevin House and as **Norman Collier** worked for them, he always did a turn. It was used for gigs only, but a regular was **Jack Barker**.

This was also T.G.W.U headquarters and it was not unusual during a lull in the proceedings to hear through a microphone. "Right, shall we vote on it brothers?" Not so bad during a dance, but the hall was also used by local amateur dramatic societies. The Hull Garret Players were doing Ibsen's 'Lady From The Sea,' when during a particularly tense moment on stage, the union members on the floor below became very raucous and the obscenities could be clearly heard in the auditorium, not at all what Mr Ibsen had in mind.

BLIND INSTITUTE

Resident for many years was Norman Mail.

Dennis Proby recalled some of the arrangements were by **Jimmy Lally**. "They were dreadful, so got slung out pronto," said Dennis

Sam Evans with his compatriots, **Eric** and **Kevin** were 'on the door'. They heard knocking but they'd been told 'we're full up, nobody else comes in.' The knocking became louder. Sam opened the door and told them in fairly flowery language, 'no admittance'. The man started to explain, but Sam was having none of that and 'smacked him one'. He lived to regret his hasty actions, it was the organiser of the dance.

Alf Stephenson, said, "The first time I ever played with **Norman Mail** was at the 'Blind'. There were two rooms, separated by an arch and it was not unusual to see Sam walking with two troublemakers under each arm and accidentally knocking their heads on the archway on the way out."

Roy Wilkin (drummer) recalls the time one of the other drummers was wearing a long blonde wig. "He thought he was attracting the girls," said Roy, "but in actual fact he looked a right pillock. But one night his sticks caught one side of the flowing locks and it squiffed over to one side, showing quite clearly his greying, balding pate to all. A huge cheer went up but it never entered his head everyone was laughing at him and blithely carried on, completely unaware of the entertainment he was offering."

The gent's was at the far end of the room, so if the band wanted a quick pee, they would go through the kitchens at the side, into the boiler room and do it outside. "There was always a huge mound of coke outside," said *Eric Wright*, "and the lads would just relieve themselves against the pile and return. One night I was doing what comes naturally when I heard a grunting, don't forget it was pitch black out there, and I could just make out this couple also doing what comes naturally. I'll give the fellah full marks," said Eric, "It was the lass who was having her head shoved into the coke."

Ray DesForges burst out laughing, "You didn't have to go outside at Beverley Road Baths to see such sights," he said, "you only had to look up at the balcony and you would invariable see a backside or two humping up and down."

Tony Richards said the Fire Brigade hired the Hall for one night each month. "I used to be on the door and and usually tore the tickets in half, gave half to the punter and put the other in my pocket, but I was told to keep the whole tickets, then about 10 pm I was informed I could then start tearing. The place was already heaving. We must have been well over the limit, but everybody was having a wonderful time."

CITY HALL

This venue would hold up to 1000 and it was full every week and like many of the other ballrooms it had a master of ceremonies, this time usually carried out by *Ron Downing*. Also as in other halls, everybody had their favourite spot.

Jay Hoyles was responsible for the catering. The musicians would rush up the four flights of stairs for sandwiches, then down again to see who could bag the best looking bird. They all looked at *Ray DesForges*. He smiled and admitted, "I know, I always won didn't I?"

In the 50's - once a year - in June - an Ideal Home Exhibition was held in this venue, which meant no dance could be held, so all the regulars would try pastures new, but soon returned to their favourite haunt. **Dr. G. Pearson** of Cottingham said that in his opinion, "All the musicians who played during this period were superb."

In 57/58/59 they tried to ban bopping as the whole floor shook alarmingly with the extreme gyrations of the dancers. But they had to give in. so the far corner, stage right, was left to the boppers while the rest carried on with strict tempo dancing.

Ken Brookes was a band leader who always wore tails, but one night, as a musician so succinctly put it, "he had the squits, and had to keep leaving the bandstand to answer the call of nature but we just carried on, even though he was the pianist. Well on one of his visits he left the tails of his suit dangling in the pan and when he returned, as always happened, before he sat down he flicked his tails over the piano seat, except this time the residue from his visit, shot up the pale cream wall behind and all over the bass player. The resulting mess I leave to your imagination."
He needn't have added that - I was way ahead!

DANCE-De-LUXE

Wow, what a chequered selection of names this establishment went under. Dancers all remembered it by a different name. Including The Palais-de-Dance, the Scala, and Albert Smith's Dance Hall.
This was a converted cinema on Anlaby Road, opened after the war by the Jack Daniels Band.
Advertised as the Palais de Danse Orchestra.
Jack himself played clarinet and piano. The rest of the line-up was: **Freddy Phillips** (piano) **Fred Marshall** (trumpet) **Eddie Bentley** (drums) **Frank Cleveland** (alto) **Bill Bailey** (tenor) **Percy Savage** (trombone) **Bill ?** (bass)
I was told they drew their repertoire from imported American recordings.
Frank Cleveland recalls the owner Albert Smith took the floor as MC. "He used to liberally powder his face. We just thought it a bit odd, but nothing more. You didn't in those days did you?"

Advert in the Hull Daily Mail
Tonights Modern Dance
8 till midnight 3/- HMF 2/-
Thurs - Old time Victory ball
7.45 - midnight 3/- HMF 2/-
FRIDAY- British Communist Party Dance
8 till midnight - 3/6 HMF 2/6

DUKE OF CUMBERLAND

The Maxwell Daniels Orchestra was one of the resident bands and was another popular venue for local dancers.

EAST PARK BALLROOM

This was built in 1940 as a decontamination centre in the event of gas attacks on the city. Part of the design brief was to make it bomb-proof. It was demolished in 2001 and there are no immediate plans for the redevelopment, but it's rumoured it might be a fish-and-chip restaurant.
It was used for many events, including boxing bouts, but the ballroom dancing fraternity still fondly remember it.

Fred Rowson's quartet played summer and winter at this popular venue. *Bert Boots* on bass.
Bert recalls the time a trio was playing there and a 'punter' came up and asked if they did requests. He was informed they did.
"Great," he said, "Can you play 'Big Noise From Winekta?"
"I don't know how the hell he was going to dance to that."

Eric Wright said: "I gigged there quite regularly with *Frank Wignall* (Wiggy Wade) Problem was he was a bit slow in paying out the money he owed. Well one night when he was playing at East Park, I went into the ballroom and asked for my money. 'Don't bother me now Eric, I'm working.' So, to no-one in particular I just said very loudly, 'Well I'm not going anywhere 'till I get the money I'm owed. Guess what, he reached into his top pocket and handed me the lot. Mind you he threatened never to use me again."

"Did he?" I asked.

"Do you know I don't think he did."

FLORAL HALL HORNSEA

Eric William's band was playing regularly when he had to go into hospital for a kidney operation. The band was taken over by *Colin Shakespeare* and he played for five happy years, until the decision was taken that it would be cheaper to hire a disco for the night.

I sometimes frequented the Floral Hall. I was going out with a Hull City player, *Tommy Forgan* at the time and *Brian Cripsey* another City player, was the only one with a car so it was not unusual to find five or six of us crammed into his little black A40. I suppose my claim to fame is that the boys entered me for the Hornsea Personality Girl and I won. No money prizes, just a large bouquet and ribbing for several months

FULFORD DANCE HALL, Beverley Road (Which was later re-named the New Brunswick)

This actually was some rooms in a house opened up by *Mr F. Hakeney*, but he'd done it properly. They boasted one of the best maple floors for dancing in the area also at the foot of the stage there was a mirror so dancers could watch their footwork as they danced past.

A jazz aficionado, *Mike Pinfold*, of South Cave, told me a band called 'Johnny Claes and his Clay Pigeons' regularly played at the Fulford but the Dutch man's real claim to fame was playing trumpet in a George Formby film. Mike said his drummer was an out and out exhibitionist. He answered to the wonderful name of Freddy Crump.

One of the resident bands was the *Rodger Stanton Orchestra* also *Haydn Powell. Harry Chatterton* put in an eleven piece band playing Stan Kenton type material. The line up was 2 trumpets, 4 saxes, accordion, trombone and rhythm. It included *Noel Flint* on bass, *Teddy Barker* on piano. Trumpets: *Keith Parker*, *Brian Hargrave*, and *Mick Richardson* on baritone. *Kay Garner* used to do a spot on vocals.

Mr Hakeney often would be stood at the side of the room with a stopwatch to check the band was playing the correct time. Very popular with the muso's!

Jean Ward, used to accompany her husband John to the dance hall and said she sometimes wore a yellow sweater with a stave and four notes, knitted into it. Whenever she walked nto the room, one of the trumpeters would stand up and play those four notes.

They also used to have a 'Jazz Club' on a Sunday and most of the local musicians would come down for a blow, with *Joanne Richardson* on vocals. When she told them she was soon to be twenty-one, the band suggested having the party at the dance hall.

"It was a really great night," said Joanne, "All the boys came forward and handed me a present. Twenty-one of them, ALL powder compacts!"

Typical of an advert in the local press:
FULFORD, Beverley Rd. - May 8th, 1945.
TONIGHT VE DANCE 8 to 1.30am 5/- and 3/-
Tomorrow Night - GRAND GALA DANCE 8 to 12 4/6 and 2/6
Afternoon Dances 2.30 to 5 1/6 and 1/-
Dancing to HAYDN POWELL and his FULL BAND.
Wonder what it was like with half a band?

GRANGE PARK HOTEL

This was a popular venue for dinner dances. There were several residencies including *Sounds Easy* and *Norman Mail*.

HESSLE TOWN HALL

Residency in the 30's and 40's was by *Ambrose Gibbins*, followed by *Harry Chatterton*. A two-year residency was taken by *Maxwell Daniels*. *Eric Wright* (drummer) said: "There was a morgue at the back, but it didn't stop punters trying to climb up and make an unscheduled entrance through a rear window."

JACKSON'S BALLROOM (Paragon St.)

This was a restaurant and ballroom over Jackson's store in Paragon Street. It became one of the busiest venues in Hull for dinner dances and luncheon clubs. Years later it became known as the White Rose Restaurant, but that closed in 1982 and became a suite of solicitor's offices.

The correct date of the original opening seems lost in the mists of time. **Bert Boots** swears it was in 1947. But a couple of other musicians were as adamant that it was 1951.

The first resident band was **Alan Bond** (alias Bert Boots, bass player) and His Music.
Vocals were produced by the **Mellow Maids, Wynn Hickey, Pat Hickey** and **Sheila Edkins.**
Line up as follows. Piano: **Bill Edkins.** Trumpet: **Len Hunter.** Alto:**Roy Longbottom.**
Tenor: **Norman Horsefall.** Drums: **Bert Hickey.**

Sheila recalls the time **Len Hunter** got dressed up as lady, to sing a duet with her.
"We were in full flow singing, 'I can do anything better than you," she said, "when Len, who was giving it his all, tripped over the hem of his dress and as near as dammit fell off infamous ashtray in which we played. He grabbed hold of the curtains and managed to heave himself back. Trouble was as we were fifteen feet up no-one noticed a thing."
Wynn Hickey added, "The worst bit was that, the public had to use the stage area, which was positively minute, as a route to the loos. There was hardly room for us and it really made for an interesting night as punters climbed over the drums. But as Sheila said, "we were high above the dancers nobody thought anything about it."

The musicians were usually given refreshments, often meat pies. One week *Alf Stephenson* noticed the pies had a date on them, which confirmed they were a week old. There was hell on," said Alf.

KEVIN BALLROOM, Market Place, Hull

Opened by *Roy Tilley* in 1960, it was the first purpose built ballroom in Hull, most of it built by Mr Tilley himself. At the end of a week playing, he would go back stage and pay the musicians in threepenny bits!

John Carnazza said: "Roy Tilly's orchestrations were brilliant, he was a real innovator."

"And not just his orchestrations," said *Paul Shepherdson*. "He used to think a good idea to get the band to forsake the stage and play in the middle of the dance floor."

There used to be a late night jazz club at the Kevin, called 'The Birdland Club', which would start at 11pm and go on until the early hours. Some of the regular musicians included:

Piano: *Eric Smith*. Bass: *John Carnazza, Noel Flint*. Drums: *Paul Shepherdson, Pete Bossen*.

Tenor: *Len Rangely*. Alto: *Ev Snowden, Brian Suttill*.

Paul Shepherdson said he remembered the drummer called *Pete Bossen*. "He was the double of Winston Churchill and he deliberately dressed to enhance the image, including cigar and homburg hat."

He also recalled *Dave Mitch* a trumpeter, who used to put draught Bass, his favourite brew, into a whisky bottle and nobody could understand why he was still standing after swigging the whole bottle.

"Another trumpeter used to do a similar thing," said Paul. "He liked a swig of beer after a solo and kept a bottle near his seat. One night one of the lads swapped the contents for soapy water. He spit it out violently and made the most almighty racket. Do you know the audience never even noticed. But it got worse, he dropped his trumpet on the floor and bent it.

"Talking about broken instruments, we were once playing on a float in the Hull Rag Parade and the bass player was stood near the back. He fell off and crashed on top of his bass. It was reduced to matchwood."

Paul also told me in the early 60's one member of the band had a motor bike, "and he gave two of us a lift. A copper stopped us. We must have looked a sight. Three fellah's on one bike, all in evening dress and shooting out from all angles a trumpet, a tenor and a trombone. He just checked who we were, then told us to be careful."

"Any more travelling stories?"

"Well in the early 60's we were playing at the Kevin and after unloading all the gear we decided the car was parked legally and carried on with the gig. When we came outside at 2am we found it had been towed away by the police. It cost us two pounds, ten shillings (2.50) to get it back".

But it all came to an abrupt end. One night the musicians turned up and found not a stick of furniture in the place, also all their kit was missing. The bailiffs had impounded it.

LOCARNO, Ferensway, Hull

Mecca opened this venue in September 1961. It was Hull's first post-war ballroom and cost £200,000. It could accommodate 2,000 people and the dance floor, costing £4,000 was specially cushioned to give dancers a unique experience.

A celebration ball and champagne supper for 800 guests was held at the opening and the first dance was held on Saturday 16th September 1961.

Donny Keith the vocalist at the time told me, "As well as the revolutionary revolving bandstand, the ceiling contained over a thousand lights."

The out of town professional band, *Ivor Kirchin* opened it, and for playing in the interval they booked *The Steve Maxwell Trio*.

There was something available every night. Mondays, was dancing to records, Tuesdays, Bingo and *Fred Ashworth*, the band's drummer was elected to be the caller, then Wednesday to Sunday the big band took the stage to play for dancing.

Admission was eight shillings (40p).

Their advertising slogan was ' Memories are made with Mecca - of course!'

MAJESTIC BALLROOM, Witham

In 1960/61 the owner bought *Eric Delaney's* pad for £900, to use by *Alan Hurst*, an outside professional band he'd brought in to open the venue. This was in the fifties, so that was a fair amount of money.

Regular dances were held three nights a week. Gradually semi-pro's were introduced. The baritone player, *Mick Richardson*, gave a grin when I asked how he'd got the job in the band. "*Alan Hurst* rang me to say his normal band member had gone sick and wouldn't be returning. I found out from the rest of the lads that he'd died of alcoholic poisoning!"

Eventually *The Harry Chatterton Orchestra* was asked to play on a regular basis.

Attendances fell alarmingly when a polio epidemic swept the country and people elected to stay indoors, plus the locarno Ballroom on Ferensway opened. Inevitable closure followed.

The line-up I was given included: Piano, *Gordon Findlay*, Bass, *John Carnazza*.

Drums, *Don Murray*.

Trumpets: *Dave Mitch*, *Wally Ingram*.

Alto: *Gordon Roberts*

Kay Garner was the highly capable vocalist, who eventually went to London to find fame and fortune as a session singer.

METROPOLE DANCE HALL (Prospect St./West St)

Resident was the *George Wheldon Dance Band* who was renowned for playing 'hot' rhythm. He also had a reputation for composing many of the original numbers. It was destroyed in the blitz and now Woolworths stands on the site.

NEWINGTON HALL, Albert Ave.

It was built in 1911 by a Mr Vokes.

At its inception it appears the downstairs area was primarily used for holding firms dinners and upstairs was a small room with a five-piece band run by an 18yr old *Harold Dawson*.

Later when it was turned solely into a dance hall, it was run by *Jack Taylor* a boxing promoter and bookie, who also played for rugby for Hull Kingston Rovers and *George Lawson* an ex-boxer and wrestler.

One of the musicians told me Lawson used to swim daily in the open-air baths in Albert Avenue, a few doors up from the dance hall.

Typical advert in the Hull Daily Mail - May 8th 1945
DANCING TONIGHT 8 to 1.30am
Ad. 5/- HMF (in uniform) 3/-
TWO BANDS - NON-STOP
Old tyme with O.G's Band. Modern - The Newington Orchestra
SWINGTIME Wed - 8 to 12
Ad. 3/6 HMF in uniform 2/6

Dances were held regularly 8 to 12, with Wednesday afternoons boasting 'Swingtime'

Just after the war, regular 'jam sessions' were held there. It included *Ted Barker* (piano) *Ted Southern* (electric guitar) *Alf Joliff* (drums) *Frank Wade/Jimmy Lucas* (bass) *Tom Sykes, Billy Clutterbrook* (trumpet) *Les Horncastle* (clarinet) *Harry Chatterton* (trombone).

Then in the late 50's a group from Hull Telephones sang at the Albert Ave. venue, calling themselves the 'Blue Notes'.

Later the line-up consisted of: Piano: *Len Baron*. Bass: *Tom Sawyer, Stan Thornham*.

Drums:*Reg. Drury, Johnny Franks*.

Saxes: *George Cox. Les Consett, Jack Rudd, Joe Klee*, who later went on to be leader of the New Zealand Symphony Orchestra.

Trombones: *Don Washbrook*.

Trumpets: *Harry Bolder, Tom Sykes*.

Guitar: *Stan Jackson, Cyril Bell*.

Vocals: *Peggy Edwards*, who later married *Tommy Fisher* and became his regular vocalist, also *Don Holden* who went on to open up an entertainment agency, Holden Enterprises. He also introduced the dances, until *Harry Brandon* came in as resident M.C.

Bernard Collinson, *Ray DesForges* and *Roy Cooper* also played at the Newington.

The band was justly considered one of the best in the area, in fact in the late 40's they won the Northern Dance Band Championship twice in a row.

Harold Dawson could be heard every Monday evening when *John Taylor* would be the guest vocalist.

Roy Cooper recalls how he had to travel to the gig by bus but there was a problem coming home. "The last bus left town at 11.30 and if we finished on time and I ran like the clappers down Albert Avenue, I could just make it, but if we over-ran by even three/four minutes, I had to walk home to Moorhouse Road."

"*Les Consett* would arrive immaculate in evening dress and climbing boots, complete with spikes. But," said Roy, "he had an identical twin brother and you'd have these weird conversations wondering why the hell he hadn't a clue what you were on about, and they never let on which you were talking to."

No alcohol was ever served at the Newington, only soft drinks and quite the most delicious home-made apple pie you've ever tasted. Men were not allowed to wear the fashionable drape jackets and it was definitely 'no admittance' if they weren't wearing a tie.

Two familiar faces would stand at the door and make sure the dress code was adhered to, *Sam Evans* and *Eric*. Sam was one of the city's most popular sportsmen and worked as a 'bouncer' in practically every local dance hall in Hull. During the 50's he had the unique distinction of being on the books of all three of Hull's top sporting teams. Hull City, Hull Football Club and Hull Kingston Rovers. By the early 60's he weighed over 18 stone and had turned his hand to wrestling. Sam was fine unless you touched his suit, then he would prove a tad difficult as he prided himself on always appearing immaculate. His compatriot Eric was big on the surface and quite frightening but at the first sign of trouble, it was Eric would do a disappearing act, leaving Sam to sort it out and he was an expert. I have seen Sam, all five foot five of him, marching through the foyer with a struggling, swearing six foot lad under each arm, the door would be opened and they would be slung unceremoniously on the street. You didn't mess with our Sam. But underneath it all he was a real pussycat and I always got a cuddle.

Eric Wright remembers another bouncer called Kevin. "Nobody dare mess with him," said Eric, "You could guarantee the hall would be trouble free if Kevin was at the door."

The Newington was at its peak in the fifties. Most of the dancers cycled to the venue. They'd built a cycle shed all along the outside of the building. You just popped the front wheel in the frame and left it. They were never locked up and as far as I know not a single bike was ever stolen. You could guarantee your trusty steed would be waiting when it was time to go home.

Ladies arrived with their wide, voluminous, circular skirts pinned around the front to stop it catching the spokes.

New Years Eve was always special at the Newington as many of the revellers would leave the dance hall and file into the nearby church, to celebrate midnight mass. Hardly any were regular churchgoers but we really enjoyed the commaderie on this special night.

During one interval, sipping lemonade and enjoying a slice of home-made apple pie, a crowd of us decided to cycle to Hornsea the following day. (Sunday) We all met in Albert Ave. Every one had second hand bikes, some were borrowed and only three boasted gears and only one pump between the lot of us.

It was a sweltering day. Three punctures later we made Hornsea, but we were all so tired we decided to eat our sandwiches, go for a paddle and head straight back to Hull. By the time we hit Coniston, most were suffering heat exhaustion, all had sunburn, and to put it mildly we were all knackered.

Over half the population cycled to work. I worked at the Trunk Exchange in Lowgate and hundreds of bikes were 'garaged' in the cellars below the Post Office. Trouble was they frequently flooded, so most of us had a pair of wellies on hand, or an obliging postman to give us a piggy-back.

The Newington provided me with my first sample of cheeky musicians. *Johnny Franks* (drummer) would unashamedly wink and smile at all the pretty girls.

Come Christmas and *George Cox*, ably assisted by *Ray DesForges*, would tie a piece of mistletoe to a long stick and wave it over the assembled throng. We needed a bit of encouragement in those days!

NEW YORK HOTEL, Anlaby Road, Hull

Many highly regarded bands played at this venue including *Harold Dawson's, New Yorkers*.

Wynn Hickey was on vocals and *Alf. Thorpe* and *Ray Lester* also were members of the band.

Teddy Barker played there for some years with a trio. *Martin Shaw* told me: "I used to cycle there with my string bass in a little cart at the back."

The *Bill Kinsey* Quartet was resident for two years. That band comprised of *Alf Stephenson* (Trumpet) *Bill Kinsey* (Keyboard) *Bert Boots* (Bass) *Larry Booth* (Drums)
Sheila Kinsey and *Ray DesForges* (Vocals)

REGAL BALLROOM, Beverley

This was one of the top venues in the area. A musician, *David Hutchins* said he'd seriousy thought about writing a book about the building as he'd started his musical career with a skiffle group called the Satellites' in the 50's. Then he formed a band called the Tremoloes', not knowing there was already a more famous group of the same name. He said he played at the Regal until 1960.

Dances every Tuesday, Friday and Saturday. The original residency was taken by a band brought in called the 'Regal Players', fronted by *Tommy Fisher*, followed by *Harry Chatterton*. In 1951/2, the ballroom was closed for floor re-surfacing. *Bill Kinsey* was offered the new contract and brought in new musicians. Harry went on to play at the Fulford Ballroom.

"One Saturday night," said **Eric Wright**, "The M.C **Bert Baker** wanted the dance to be extended by two numbers. **Bill Kinsey** (Edkins) and he were having a right old ding-dong, but unbeknown to them the mike was on and the row was being relayed throughout the building including the restaurant on the floor below. **Tom Allanson** came storming through the ballroom waving his arms. Too late everybody had heard the argument."

"Who won?" I asked.

"Can't remember. We were having too much of a giggle to care."

It had a large sign over the stage, which read. "No Jitterbugging Allowed."

A pattern was soon set. Tuesday's became 'rep's night' and on Friday's they played host to many famous guest bands.

There was also great rivalry between the ballroom and cinema managers. One night all the punters arrived for the dance only to find a giant cardboard cut-out of **Harry Secombe** next to the drums.

Len Fallowfield, a coal merchant by trade, built all the music stands for the **Bill Kinsey Band**. I was told, "They were heavy and substantial. Absolutely brilliant, especially the sax section which he'd built all in one piece in a sort of arc."

The Regal is fondly remembered by many. It was a favourite venue for the nurses at the Westwood Hospital, particularly the students, but they had a strict 11.30pm curfew. **Allan Rowlands**, the only male student among fifty girls, recalls the time four of them had paid a visit to the ballroom and suddenly realised it was 11.25pm. "They rushed for their coats and ran all the way back to the nurses home, but they were ten minutes late, the doors were locked. They saw a nearby sash window open and decided to try and climb in. They furtively checked around then girl number one, pushed through the curtains and disappeared, followed by the second then the third. Allan was number four and was half-way through the window when he was aware of someone watching - "I looked up - only to be faced with the very person we were trying to deceive. Sister!"

"I think the dance cost about five or six shillings - about 25p - said Allan, "but in those days nurses pay was pitiful and even though many of us would have loved to go to the ballroom, we couldn't afford it, so would pool our limited resources. We usually only had enough for ten Woodbine and a bottle of cider. When we were really flush, we would first go to a nearby pub, the White Horse, known as 'Nellies.' Nellie would never serve a lady with a pint glass and she refused to serve us more than two pints of 'Nellie's Old.' "We'll go somewhere else," we told her. "Yes, and I'll tell Sister." she would reply. So we were always in perfect control when we strutted our stuff at the 'Regal'.

In the centre of the dance floor was a large square, made up of several smaller squares of thick coloured glass, lit from below. If you were executing a nifty quickstep on the highly polished floor and hit the glass, you suddenly came to a grinding halt. It also had the obligatory silver ball, rotating in the centre of the ceiling.

All the girls stood at the cloakroom end, the boys well away, at the other end.

Many dancers, including myself, would leave our bikes at Hull's Paragon Station and catch the train to Beverley. The last train went at midnight, so the station was awash with couples having a quick snog before the train left.

Bert Baker the M.C was always immaculate in evening dress. I was told he was also a dance teacher. One night there was a fracas at the door and someone said to **Brian Hargrave**, "Go and get Bert." but instead of trying to locate Bert, the mild mannered Brian went to the troublemakers and sorted them out himself. They all meekly turned away and went. "What the hell did you say to them?" "Nothing much." said Brian and promptly sat and picked up his trumpet and carried on as if nothing had happened.

In 1998 the building was pulled down. Mourned by many musicians and dancers. It now lies a barren desert of rubble. Quite heartbreaking. Another link of our history bulldozed to extinction.

As a surprise, **Ray Scott's** -he played in the Kinsey Orchestra - girlfriend Lynda, went rummaging in the rubble and brought home a brick as a reminder of very special times.

ST. AIDENS

It was used regularly for dances on a Saturday night. "It was when I first started," said *Alf Stephenson*. "Every Saturday, without fail, a fight would break out. To escape the mayhem we would all have to climb over the piano, which was crammed into a corner."

They used to have two drummers, *Roy Wilkin* and *Geoff Smith*. "It was not unusual for us both to turn up," said Roy, " so we would take it in turns. They paid us £2.10 a night. I remember *Alf Stephenson* left to play with *Les Rose* for nothing. We all thought he was mad, but as Alf said, it was the best band in the town and the experience was invaluable."

Keith Parker (trumpet) said he started his musical career at St. Aidens. "I had a band called the 'Metro's'. It included *Rob Kerring* on sax. and *Barry Northmoor* on piano.

St. VINCENTS - Queen's Road, Hull

Dances were held on Mondays, Fridays and Saturdays. *Tommy Fisher* was a regular.

Advert 1945
Late night dance tonight.
Margery Dales and The Victory Four.
Mixed Programme
M.C: F.Ford ad 2/6

SKYLINE BALLROOM / BAILEYS, Jameson St. Hull

This venue was on the top floor of the old Co-operative store in George St.

It was opened by a an out of town pro. band fronted by *George Slater*, who featured on alto and soprano, with *Pattie Kane* on vocals.

Bob Grant later took up the residency

Some of the local musicians who played at the Skyline were *George Wilcox*, *Martin Shaw*, *Ray DesForges*, *Mick Richardson*, *Pete Dawson*, *Roy Cone*, *Mark Class*, *Albert Harrison* and *Jack Barker*.

In 1971 the Bailey organisation took over the premises and the Lord Mayor of Hull opened it, with numerous councillors and civic leaders. The cabaret was the singer *Judith Durham.*

Saturday evenings were devoted to a cabaret dinner-dance and the cost varied from £2 to £3, depending on the cabaret act.

It seated nearly 600 people

STATION HOTEL

Another venue where the *Bill Kinsey Quartet* was resident for dinner dances.

The same personnel as before: Keyboard: *Bill Edkins*, Bass; *Bert Boots*. Drums: *Larry Booth* Trumpet: *Alf Stephenson* Vocals: *Sheila Edkins* and *Ray DesForges.*

The 'stage' had to be erected before each session, then a carpet was placed over the boards, but it left uneven, curled edges and frequently the poor old waiters would trip over it and on several occasions the contents of their trays were spilt over unsuspecting dancers.

"In fact one night," said Sheila, "I was wearing a new white dress and I had just got up to sing the first number, when wham, over a waiter went, the contents of five glasses all spilling over my new frock. It was a real mess. I had to change and for the rest of the night I looked very fetching in a blue, floral number." She laughed. "Larry our drummer was having a good laugh, but he lived to regret it. The following week the waiter shot straight into his drum kit. The audience loved it, but Larry and the waiter were not amused."

John Carnazza recalled a night when he was playing with *Norris Walker* at an annual Jewish event and the band was playing for the diners who had just started their meal. "Suddenly," said John, " a large florid gentleman stood up and shouted to the assembled throng, ''Stop eating everyone, we're being poisoned.' As you can expect there was a great to do, but we kept on playing, while everyone rushed around like blue ***** flies. We found out later they were being served prawn cocktail. Not acceptable to the Jewish faith."

VAUXHALL. Known locally as DICK WRIGHT'S

They weren't allowed to sell liqueur, so most people drank Sunfresh orange. One lady rcalls she would drink gallons of the stuff and became known as "The Sunfresh Kid."

WESTFIELD COUNTRY CLUB

Many bands and musicians played at this establishment, including
Milner Marshall Band.
Piano: *Brian Milner*
Bass: *Dave Milner*
Drums: *Jimmy Marshall*
Tenor: *Alf Rivetts*
Vibes: *Bazz Hewland*

In the 60's and 70's, the musicians included: Piano: *George Roberts*, *Van James.*
Bass: *Pete Williams, Noel Flint.*
Drums: *Colin Berriman.*
Vocalist and compere: *Ray DesForges.*

These were the halcyon days for the club, when every top line artist in the country were guests, including: *Bruce Forsythe, Vince Hill* and *Larry Grayson.*
Roy Castle, who visited on at least seven occasions, and who *Ray Desforges* considered 'The Guv'nor', He also speaks highly of *Bob Monkhouse, Bernie Clifton, Tommy Cooper* and the late *Dustin Gee.*

An advert for May 1973 showed the talent appearing the following month included: *Peter Gordeno* and his dancers, *Charlie Williams, Jimmy Tarbuck* and *Dave Allen.*
Ken Dodd was performing there and as usual went on for an hour and a half over the allotted time. By the third night the musicians were in revolt as he refused to pay them overtime. *Keith Parker* was selected to be the band's spokesman to face Mr Dodd, but he wouldn't give way. In fact he took it as a

personal attack from Keith. About two years later Ken Dodd's agent rang Keith to ask him if he'd play at a gig he was doing at Sheffield. "He wont want me," said Keith, "He hates me." "No, it's all right," said the agent. Of all the trumpeter's in the north he hates you least."

"How about that for a back-handed compliment?" said Keith.

One of the most regular patrons in the 60's and 70's was Rt. Hon. *John Prescott* MP. He very seldom missed a Saturday night and without fail he and his wife Pauline would take the floor - and I can vouch for the nifty footwork of the Deputy Prime Minister.

Colin Crompton, of Wheeltappers & Shunters Club' and 'The Comedians' wrote a letter to the Hull Daily Mail after many visits.

"I have appeared at the Westfield many times. It has exciting musicians who would outshine any professional on any variety bill. First class working conditions and owners who take a personal interest.

The Wheeltappers and Shunters club image is thankfully numbered. We are continuing on telly, but give me the Westfield anytime."

Other musicians who played at the Westfield included: *Stuart Day, Eric Chapman, Ken Cook, Pete Parker, Roy Cooper, Ronnie Wray, Martin Obidans, Colin Wood, Keith Stutt* and *Eric Seaward.*

WEST PARK BALLROOM

Harry Chatterton opened the club with his band in the 1960's.
Later it was often used as a venue for the MU workshops, run by *Leslie Rose.*

WILLERBY MANOR HOTEL

Frank Cleveland was resident at the hotel and he told me a story about when the hotel decided to enlarge the dance area. "We arrived one night to find the whole of the back wall had been knocked down, with only a tarpaulin covering the hole. "I've never been so cold in my life," said *Ricky Cleveland.*

Eric Wright the drummer vividly recalls the entrance for the musicians, "The whole thing was a sea of mud. We used to go in goloshes it was so bad. One night one of the punters had had a bit too much to drink and was feeling the worse for wear, so I took him outside, while he was leaning against the door I fetched a chair and sat him in it. 'Wait there and I'll get your coat,' I told him. While I was gone he'd attempted to stand and zonk, face first in the mud. He just lay there. You should have seen him, it was disgusting, mud was dripping from everything."

WINDSOR HALL, Anlaby Road (corner Argyle St.)

This was a long wooden building with mirrors all along wall. I was told it was to make it look bigger. *Teddy Barker* ran the Students Union Orchestra, playing arrangements which are still used by the musicians in the 90's, also many of the musicians today started off in with *Teddy Barker*. Players which were in that student orchestra are still working in the Hull area.

Griff Williams (drummer) was the librarian.

Some MU clinics, run by *Leslie Rose* were held here and *Eddie Grey*, from the Kirchin Band, did many arrangements for them.

A regular date was Sunday morning with *Teddy Barker* piano, *Ted Southern*, guitar, *Alf Joliff* Drums, *Frank Wade* and *Timmy Lucas* who took turns at bass. *Tom Sykes* & *Billy Clutterbrook* trumpet, *Les Horncastle* clarinet, *Harry Chatterton*, trombone.

Paul Shepherdson said he'd been playing there, "and coming home there were a gang of us all crammed in a car, including the instruments. We over-steered on a corner and my arm shot forward, smashing through the bass drum skin."

WITHERNSEA GRAND PAVILION

The first residency was held by *Tommy Fisher*, with a line up of five saxes, three trumpets and three trombones. *Ken Hawkins* was on drums, *Jack Sheard*, bass. Trumpets included, *Wally Ingram*, and *Dave Mitchell*. *Roy Cooper* was on trombone and *Percy Stather*, saxophone.

It was open every night with some sort of entertainment and was a particularly popular venue for dancers from around the region, boasting 'we have the largest sprung floor in Northern England.'

On Saturday nights the hall would be packed, as special trains would be laid on from Hull. Often after a dance the revellers would all congregate on the beach and organise a party around bonfire.

Y.P.I.

I was informed by *Trevor Singleton*, a devotee of the dance halls in the 1950's and 60's, that *Louis Gold and his Monarchs of Melody* were resident at the above venue.

Heat of Come Dancing, Locarno Ballroom Hull

Come Dancing, Locarno Ballroom

The Alan Bond Band at Jacksons' Ballroom 1951

City Hall 1956/57

Vi Clarke was a familiar figure at the City Hall, taking photographs to record the occasion.
L/R Tony Richards, Betty Richards, Dorothea Rankin, John Rankin 1958

White House Swingtette
L/R: Harold Dawson, ?, Fred Rawson, Jacky Lee

Jacksons' Ballroom, City Engraving Dance

Regal Ballroom, Beverley

Withernsea Pavilion

George Wilcox

Beverley Regal 1960
L/R: Ray Desforges, George Spicer, Ray Scott, John Grindley

IN THE PIT AT THE THEATRE

Many of the musicians play at the local theatre for musicals or pantomime so I couldn't resist asking for some stories.

Dixon Laing recalls the time he was in the pit for a production of 'Jesus Christ Superstar,' "The musical director was as pompous as they come. At the dress rehearsal he marched into the pit, stood on his little dais, held his arms out wide and loudly tapped his baton on the music stand, 'Can everyone see me? Asked the musical director. Quick as a flash the drummer said: 'Who said that?' The whole band collapsed with laughter, but the M.D was not amused."

Dixon also told me, "Another musician was so full of his own importance that at dress rehearsal he complained bitterly that the piano stool was cold. For the rest of the week, he insisted that somebody sat on it for half-an-hour before he went on."

Alf Stephenson recalled the time he was playing for the panto at Hull New Theatre and someone asked, "Have you seen who's in the box tonight lads?"
"No who?"
"That comedian, *Freddy 'Parrot face' Davies*."
Quick as a flash, *Keith Parker* muttered, 'Well close the bloody lid before he escapes, I can't stand him."

Les Dennis was a popular act with the musicians. "We managed to corpse him every night," said Alf, "but he got his own back. On the third night he came on with brand new shoes, he headed to the edge of the stage and stood with his soles over the edge on full display to the boys in the pit. He's written 'F*** off,' on them. The audience must have thought we were all mad as the whole pit heaved with uncontrollable laughter."

Paul Shepherdson said: "*Lawrence Rugg*, a highly regarded M.D, was playing for the Northern Theatre's show, 'William Wilberforce'. He decided it would be interesting to re-arrange the national anthem in the style of the period. But there was a problem, it sounded so obscure the audience hadn't a clue it was being played so stayed firmly in their seats. It was changed for the rest of the run."

His wife Sandra smiled. "At a matinee of Sweet Charity, Lawrence decided to play the number 'Big Spender' at double tempo. I managed, but was in a heap at the end of the number. I asked him why. 'I thought it might be fun,' he told me."

She continued: "In one show **Maggie North** had skipped some of her vocals and when we looked in the pit, there were all the poor musicians madly flipping through the music trying desperately to find where she was.

"But I think what was even worse was when we were doing 'Threepenny Opera' at Spring Street Theatre. At dress rehearsal, we had got through two verses of a number and couldn't recall what followed. We asked Jonathan the M.D what was next. 'Don't ask me,' he said, 'The whole score's in German."

Let's finish this chapter with a story from **Norman Baron**. When I asked him if he'd ever played in the theatre he replied, "Stacks of times. In fact on one show there was a juggler on stage - not a very good one either - He was tossing around balloons, Indian clubs and for some unknown, bizarre reason, Barbi Dolls, but worst of all were the metal balls. The bloody things started spinning completely out of control and were shooting into the pit. I likened it to being under siege from cannon balls. First one hit the bass player on the head, another bounced alarmingly off a snare drum and a third hit the keyboard player in a very tender spot. His scream brought the act to a shuddering halt."

As I said: "Would you like your balls back, takes on a completely new connotation."

COMMENTS FROM DANCERS
OF THE ERA

Mrs Savage said in 1953 when she was eighteen, she was going to the City Hall. "It was my first ball and my aunt had told me to cut my hair as it made it thicker, so I decided to snip the tips off my eyelashes. To complete the look I smeared them with my father's black boot polish instead of mascara.

Arriving at the dance, my eyes became so sore from the smoky atmosphere that I completely forgot about the boot polish and started to rub them. Needless to say I had to leave the dance early in floods of tears and a very smudgy face."

Mike Pinfold of South Cave says he recalls most of the dance halls putting up a rope to segregate dancers who wanted to 'bop'. "You only had to stray a few feet and a voice would yell, 'Get behind that rope'.

Marie Fitzgerald of Hathersage Rd, Hull said she started dancing at St. Vincent's, then in the mid-fifties she frequented the Newington on Albert Avenue.

"I loved the atmosphere and Don the singer was special too. There was a door on the ballroom, which led into a small garden, where couples would slip out for a quick cuddle. Don't forget these were the days of no sex before marriage, so a quick snog was all on offer. We all used to wait to be asked to go in it, and if we weren't asked, we watched intently to see who the lucky ones were. I regard those days at the Newington the best days of my life.

"After getting to know most people there, the regulars who didn't have boyfriends or girlfriends used to go to the Kardomah café on a Saturday afternoon and Regal Cinema on a Sunday evening.

"I also went to the Blind Institute, Beverley Road Baths, East Park ballroom and ending up at the City Hall. I met my husband there.

"All the girls wore full gathered skirts and hooped underskirts, in fact we starched our petticoats with sugar to make them stand out more.

"When we got on the bus we had to sit on the long seat at the back, because when you sat down the hoops shot upwards and anyway they wouldn't fit in the ordinary seats."

Mrs Betty Richards of Westbourne Avenue, said she left school at 14 and a cousin asked if she wanted to go to a dance. "My mother said no way, but my cousin wrote her a letter promising her she would look after me, so she relented. We walked there and on our return all stayed together in my cousins house, going home the next day. The three of us slept together in one bed. We thought the musicians were brilliant. They were such special times and I'll never forget them".

"They were great days," admits *Dr G. Pearson*, Mill Walk, Cottingham.

"I also spent most Saturday nights at the Newington Hall dancing to the Newington Orchestra Sometimes we'd go to the Regal Ballroom, Beverley and dance to Tommy Fisher, also to Jacksons Ballroom and Len Ibson. Hull had some great bands but I thought the Newington was superb."

Mrs Barbara Bayston of Hull, says: "I still hold a great affection for the dance hall days, particularly the Danse de Luxe, where I met my husband".

Mrs Marjorie Brentano of Sutton, said when she saw that Jackson's Ballroom was being converted, lots of wonderful memories came floating back.

"I always look up at the windows when I pass Jackson's and think of the lovely times we had working there and the ballroom dancing was really special. Len Ibson was the staff manager and he used to run a band which played on Saturday afternoons."

Nancy Latus of Broomfleet. "In the late 50's, early 60's I went dancing 5 or 6 nights a week mainly the Newington, City Hall and Beverley Regal. I used to make my own dresses and wore a different one every night. I would wear it once, then sell it to one of my workmates at the G.P.O. Telephone Exchange.

They were unforgettable times. All the girls used to put their handbags under a chair and there they'd stay. No-one had anything stolen and we never, ever drank alcohol. Very, very special times".

Mr A. E. Green of Priory Rd., Hull. "I first went to the Dance-de-Luxe, which we all called the Scala. Albert Smith the owner lived in a bay-window house to the left of the Scala. He always made the announcements. I vividly remember, before we took to the dance-floor, standing underneath pale blue arches."

Joan Fellows, from Molescroft said she thoroughly enjoyed visits to the Danse-de-Luxe, Fulford and the Newington Hall. "There were plenty of partners in those days, everyone was there for one thing. To have a jolly good evening's dancing, which we did.

I even met my future husband there when I was nearly eighteen and we were married for nearly fifty happy years. He didn't even ask me to dance until he'd been introduced to me! Not like that today is it?

How grateful that I lived through those 'Golden Dancing Years,' - Wonderful."

The perfect note to end on.

Questions for musicians

The following questions can be attributed to any instrument, but on one particular night it was a trumpet player who was the but of them all.

Q. Why does the chicken cross the road? A. To get away from the trumpet player.
Q. How many trumpeters does it take to change a light bulb? A. Only one, but he'll do it too loudly.
Q. What do trumpet players use for birth control? A. Their personalities.
Q. What do you call a lead trumpet with half a brain? A. Gifted.

This poor hapless musician was not amused and when the dance was over he rushed outside, climbed into his battered old Morris Minor and headed for the pier, leaving his trumpet on the road. Without stopping he drove headlong into the local horse wash. Except the tide was out and he was rescued. It was headline news in the Hull Daily Mail.

The musician in question ended up apologising to the band telling them that, he didn't mean to cause them any upset and he didn't blame them. "He said he understood we didn't mean it personally, but we laid off him after that."

Anyway here's a few I thought you might like:

We'll start with the poor mis-understood DRUMMERS:
What do you call someone who hangs out with musicians?
A drummer.

And did you about the time a bass player lost the keys to his car?
It took two hours to get the drummer out.

Now let's move to the SAXOPHONE.
How do you get two soprano saxophones to play in unison?
Shoot one.

What's the difference between a saxophone and a chainsaw?
Vibrato.

Do you know why we have so much trouble with air pollution in the world?
Most of it has passed through saxophones.

TROMBONE:
What's the difference between a dead snake in the road and a dead trombonist?
The skid marks are before the snake.

What is the difference between a dead trombone player lying in the road and
a dead squirrel lying in the road?
The squirrel might have been on his way to a gig.

What kind of calendar does a trombone player use for his gigs?
Year-at-a-glance.

GUITAR.
How do you get a guitarist to play quiet?
Put music in front of him.

BANJO.
What is perfect pitch?
When, from a distance, you can throw a banjo into a toilet bowl without
hitting the rim.

What's the difference between a banjo and a guitar?
Banjos burn longer.

TRUMPET.
What's the difference between trumpet players and Government bonds?
Government bonds eventually mature and earn money

CLARINET.
What is the difference between a clarinet and an onion?
Nobody cries when they chop a clarinet up into little pieces.

FRENCH HORN.
Why is the French horn a divine instrument?
Because a man blows in it, but only God knows what comes out of it.

VOCALIST.
How does a girl vocalist change a lightbulb?
She holds it. The rest of the world revolves around her.
So to outraged of Atwick, Bilton, Cave, Doncaster, etc., etc., etc., etc..
Please feel free to amend to the male gender.

Alan Plater and John Prescott - well known jazz enthusiasts

TAIL-PIECE

The Deputy Prime Minister, John Prescott, expressed a desire to write the foreword to this book as he and his wife Pauline love dancing. He says it's the perfect way to relax.

The date he accepted my invitation was the 10th September 2001, so as you can imagine Mr Prescott soon had much more on his mind than writing a few words for a local publication.

I first met Mr Prescott and his wife at the Westfield Country Club where every Saturday for several years, they enjoyed a pleasant evening out, taking every opportunity to take to the dance floor.

Music has always been an important part of John's life, particularly the dance band and without doubt he mourns the passing of an era.

John Carnazza - 1952
Playing 'Cumana' - a very fast Samba at the Paris Cinema, Haymarket, London
for Opportunity Knocks

Fulford Hall, Beverley Road, Hull 1975 - Proprietor F Hakeney

From L/R: Bill Edkins, Piano - Bill Pickles, Bass - Bert Hickey, Drums - Harry Robb, Trombone

From L/R: Roy Longbottom, Teddy Barker, Vic Cheeseman, Les Jordan, Ken Ormston

Adelaide Club 1957 - Tpts: Trevor Hickson, Billy Clutterbrook; Piano: Eric Smith; Bass: John Carnazza; Drums: Sammy Walsham; Vocals: Ted Flint.

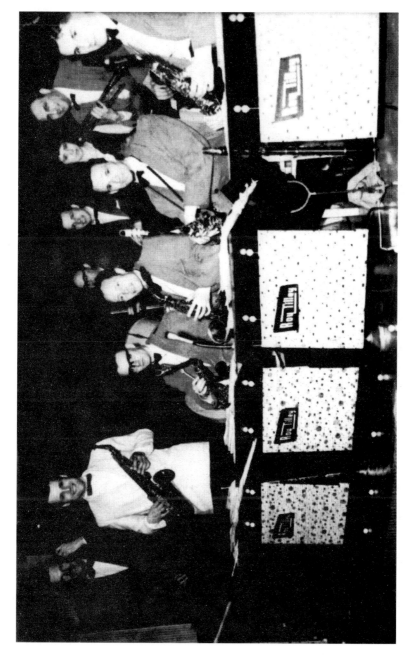

Kevin Ballroom 1960 - The Roy Tilley Band

Kay Garner at the Adelaide Club - 1959

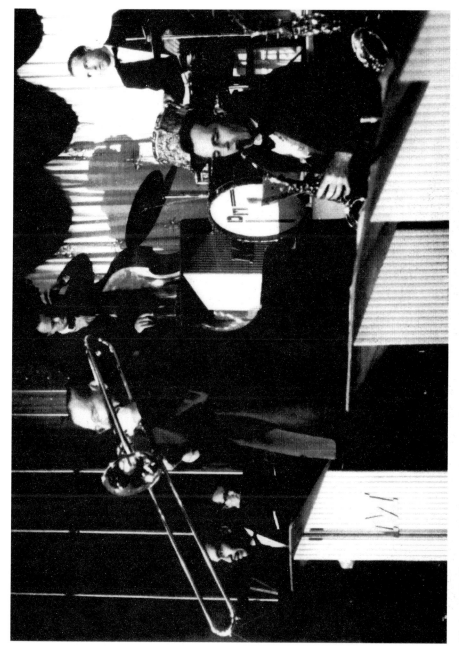

Majestic Ballroom, Witham - 1960/61; YL/R: Vocailst: Leon Riley; Pianist: Gordon Findlay; Trombone: Harry Chatterton; Bass: John Carnazza; Saxophone: Gordon Roberts; Drums: Don Murray.

John Carnazza at the New York Hotel- Late 1950's with Teddy Barker

A signed cartoon of the legendary Four Freshmen who appeared at the Westfield Country Club. After the show they accepted Ray Scott's invitation to his home. After 2 hours of sparkling conversation with just a handful of local musicians they returned to their hotel in Beverley.

A signed photograph of the legendary Oscar Peterson, given to Ray DesForges after entertaining a spellbound audience at the Westfield Country Club.

CONCLUSION

On behalf of a generation of terpsichorean talent, may I say to all the musicians Thanks for the memory.

BANDS FROM THE SWINGING YEARS

Barker Teddy
Barker Jack
Blue Rhythm Swingtette
Bond Alan
Brown Mike
Cecil Theatre Band
Chatterton Harry
Cleveland Frank
Crackajacks
Cross Mickey
Daniels Maxwell
Dawson Harold
Fisher Tommy
Fledglings
Franks Johnny
Gibbins Ambrose
Gold Louis
Harper Ceres & Edwin
Hopper Harry
Hurst Alan
Jazz Vehicle
Ibson Len
Kingston Saxophone Quartet
Kinsey Bill
Kirchin Ivor
Laycock Geoff
Lester Ray
Mail Norman
Manley Les
Mayo Gene
New Yorkers
Pinkney Graham

Rose Leslie
Shakespeare Colin
Sioux City Seven
Sounds Easy
Three Blind Mice
Walker Norris
Wright Eric Trio
White House Swingtette

VENUES

Adelaide Club
Assembly Rooms
Beverley Rd Baths
Blind Inst.
Cave Castle
City Hall
Danse de Luxe Anlaby Rd (also known as Palais de Danse)
Duke of Cumberland
East Park
Farmery Hall(Bevin House) George St Hull
Floral Hall Hornsea
Fulford, Beverley Rd.
Grange Park Hotel, Willerby.
Hessle Town Hall
Jacksons Ballroom,
Kevin Ballroom, Market Place
Locarno, Ferensway, Hull.
Majestic Ballroom, Witham
Metropole Dance Hall
Newington Hall, Albert Avenue.
New York
Regal Ballroom, Beverley
St. Aidens
St. Vincents
Skyline Ballroom, Jameson St.
Station Hotel
Vauxhall (Dick Wrights)
Westfield Country Club, Cottingham.
West Park
Willerby Manor Hotel
Windsor Hall
Withernsea Pavilion
Y.P.I

ABOUT THE AUTHOR

Dorothea lives in East Yorkshire with her husband Ray.

She owned two successful travel agencies but ill health forced her to take early retirement. She then started a new career as an author and has had several short stories published, plus six books.

These are mostly anecdotal and taken from some of the extraordinary people she met in her kaleidoscopic life.

OTHER BOOKS

Buttocks, Boobs & Bedpans:
A comic look at the medical profession and their patients in Hull and East Yorkshire. (With numerous cartoons)
£6.99

The Shocking Truth:
Another humorous insight into the lives of Yorkshire folk. Weird, wonderful and downright barmy, as seen though the eyes of a market researcher. (With cartoons)
£6.99

Travel, the Celebrity Way:
Anecdotes from 130 well-known famous personalities, including: Rolf Harris, Matthew Kelly, Richard Branson, John Nettles, Bob Monkhouse and John Prescott MP.
Hysterical honeymoons, cocky camels, paralytic porters, galloping goats and broken bones. It's all there and a lot more as well.
£6.99

Beyond The Brave:
Follow three Hull brothers as they battle with bears, blizzards and buffalo. A powerful portrayal of Canadian pioneers, 1880-1946. (With photographs)
£7.40

The In-Between Years 1940-1945
With a label around her neck a six-year-old girl was catapulted from her inner city home to a remote wheat farm in Canada. Follow her five extraordinary years in the Canadian Prairies. (With photographs)
£7.00

Books only available at: Waterstones Bookshop, Jameson St., Hull,
Brown's Books, George St. Hull
Or by post from
Buttercup Press, Ferry Road, South Cave, East Yorkshire, HU15 2JG
Cheques payable to D. Desforges.
Please add £1.40 P & P (UK only)